ANNAPŪRṆĀ

About the Author

Dr. (Mrs.) P. Arundhati, M.A. Ph.D. is presently working as an Administrative Officer in the Archaeological Survey of India, New Delhi. As a Registering officer in the department she discovered several sites and temples of archaeological significance. She keeps herself engaged in academic pursuits with her wanted scholarship and sensitivity.

Her earlier work "Brāhmanism, Jainism and Bhuddhism in Āndra Dēsa", "Royal life in Mānasôllāsa" and "Choreography in Mānasôllāsa" are rich contribution to Indological studies. She is Life Member of many learned bodies in India like Indian History Congress, Musuem Association of India, Indian Archaeological Association and Andhra Pradesh History Congress.

ANNAPŪRṆĀ

A Bunch of Flower of Indian Culture

DR. (Mrs.) P. ARUNDHATI

CONCEPT PUBLISHING COMPANY, NEW DELHI-110059

ISBN : 81-7022-897-2

First Published 2001

Published and Printed by
Ashok Kumar Mittal
Concept Publishing Company
A/15-16, Commercial Block, Mohan Garden
New Delhi-110059

Phones : 5648039, 5649024
Fax : 091-11-5648053
Email : publishing@conceptpub.com

Dedicated

to

My Husband

Sri. C.V. Subba Rao

PREFACE

Annapūrṇā is a bunch of flowers that bloomed in my academic life since I joined Ph.D. as research student in 1966.

The sprouts of these articles have shooted forth after my marriage, therefore, I feel that my husband who has been giving his cooperation to me deserves to be the receiver of this bouquet as a token of my respect for him.

The mistakes noted, if any, may kindly be tolerated by the reader.

I hope that Annapūrṇā will evoke streams of mental nourishment to the readers.

New Delhi
July 18, 2000

P. ARUNDHATI

ACKNOWLEDGEMENTS

Annapūrṇā fascinated me on those days when I was Assistant Curator, State Museum, Govt. of Andhra Pradesh. The sculpture of Annapūrṇā was exhibited at that time in the centre, at the entrance of Museum building and as a result, in variably I had to look at the figure before the museum doors were opened.

Thus, I wrote my article on Annapūrṇā and read it in a seminar during the South Indian Archaeological Association in year 1979 and it was highly appreciated by scholars. That gave me a fresh inspiration to expand my thoughts on different branches of knowledge.

I am obliged to acknowledge the Commissioner, Dept. of Archaeology and Museum, Govt. of Andhra Pradesh for permitting me to use the photograph of Annapūrṇā image.

I am greteful to Smt. Komal Anand I.A.S. Director General, Archaeological Survey of India for permitting me to use the photograph of Gudimallam Siva Linga and the photograph of Harappan seal.

I am thankful to Shri Ch. Vidya Sagara Rao, Hon'ble Minister for Home Affairs Government of India and his wife Smt. Vinoda Rao, Shri Yerram Naidu, Hon'ble Member of Parliament Lok Sabha and his wife Smt. Vijaya for giving me moral support to continue may research. I am indebted to Shri M. N. Deshpande, former Director General, Archaeological Survey of India, Prof. Dr. Ajay Mitra Shastri, Nagpur University and Dr. S.R. Rao well known Marin Archaeologist; and to Smt. Renu Sharma and Smt. Rani Sharma who constantly encourage me to take up new topics for research.

Last but least are my family members who stood by me all through thirty years of my research work.

I am thankful to Smt. Rajni Prasad and Shri S.K. Sharma who read the script and to Shri Ashok Mittal who published Annapūrṇā and presented to the readers.

CONTENTS

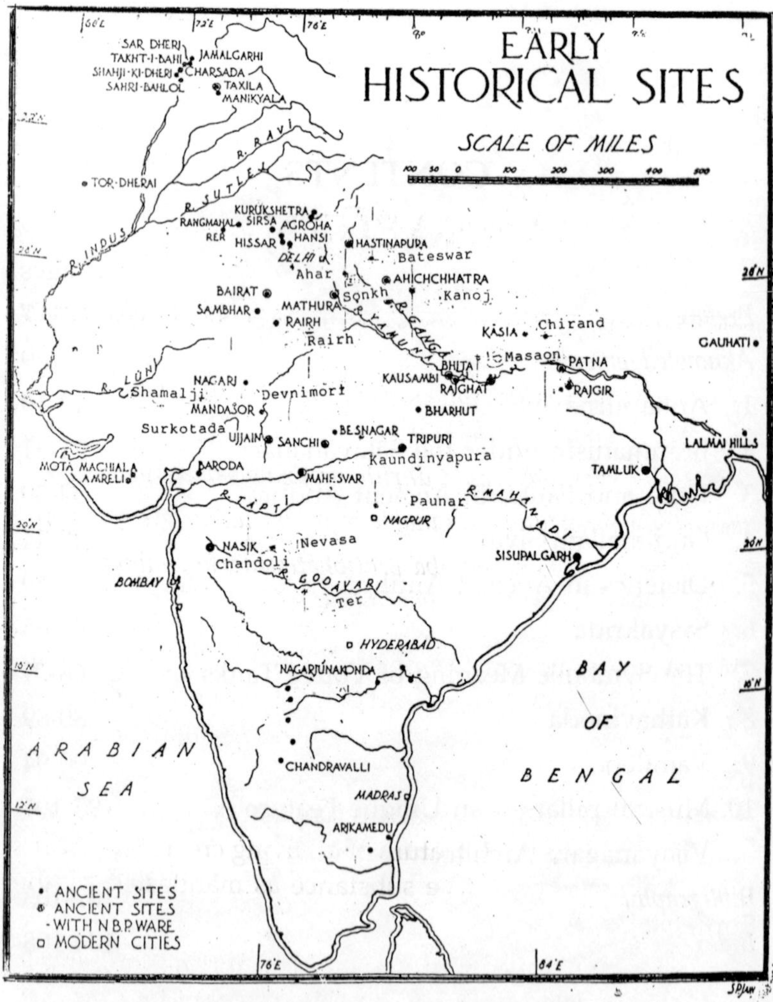

Map : Early Historical site include Amarāvati as an N. B. P. ware site.

1

ANNAPŪRṆĀ

"Vamē mānikya pātram madhurarasabharitam bibhratīm pāṇipadme·
divyairanyaih prapūrṇam dhṛutamaṇivalaye dakṣiṇe darvīm
raktāṁgīm pīnattuṅga sthanabharamitām tārahoarôpa sēvyām
vaṅdē pūrṇendubiṁba pratibhatavadanāmaṁbika mannapūrṇām"

The term Annapūrṇā (female gender) is derived from sanskrit root 'ad', to eat, the noun form of which is "Annaṁ" which is eaten; and the neutar gender is 'Anna', food.

The cult of mother goddess has its origin in food and nourishment, the basic feature of all living creatures. 'Anna' is the lowest or primitive substance as manifested by the Supreme Soul.

All ancient civilizations yielded terracotta female figurines depicted with full breasts or as holding breasts; as bedecked with innumerable ornaments or as nude. These are classified as the figures of Mother goddesses worshipped for nourishment and fertility.

Sir John Marshall found at Mohenjodaro many female figurines which had been identified as mother goddesses. (Mackay's Indus Civilization). One figure of a nude female issuing plant from her womb was found at Harappa also (Marshall's *Mohenjodaro and Indus Civilization*, Vol. I p.52, PL-XII).

The cult of mother goddess is expressed in different froms in ancient Indian literature. In the Vēdas, Goddess Aditi is called the Divine mother as she brings forth all life; and since from her springs the life. She is boundless, realmless, supporter of sky and sustainer of all (Macdonell's *Vedic Mythology*, p. 120-124). Prithvi, another goddess is called mother earth, known for her benefaction, fortitude, gentle qualities and kindness. She is called consort of father Dyus (sky). Goddesses Sīta and Gauri are the other deities associated with agriculture, presiding over the furrow of the field and crops respectively. The goddesses Āpah (Waters) was also prayed for nourishment by the vedic seers, while the goddess Āraṇyāṇi was prayed for protection from cruel animals in the forest. Besides, Sôma, Uṣas, Rākā, Kuhū, Anumatī, Sinīvālī (the Goddess presiding over vanning and waxing of moon-health) were also known to sages of the Vedic period.

In Āraṇyakas, Amṛta, Rasa, Pīyūṣha, Baıa, Puṣthi, (nourishment & strength) are attributed to the goddess Lakṣmī. In the *Śatapatha Brāhmaṇa* and *Atharva vēda*, Durga is called Annapūrṇā or Annadhātri who is represented by evergrowing food or nourishment and as offerer of food, while Agni, Savita, Sāvitṛ and Viṣṇu; are called "Annapati" (Lord of food). Annapatni, the goddess presiding over food is also referred to in the texts. The Aiterēya Brāhmaṇa, the Āśvalāyana sūtras and the Śatapatha Brāhmaṇa refer to Annapralaya-dissolution into food.

In Mahābhārata, 'Annabhāja' is referred to as one of the names of Śiva. The epics praise Bhūdēvi, the goddess of earth, and Śākambharī, one of the forms of Durga, (P. Kumar's *Śakticult* p.33). The Buddhists refer to the goddess Vasudhārā as presiding over earth and crops. Coming to the puranic period, Dēvimāhātmya of Mārkandēyapurāṇa describes Dēvi as Śākāmbharī who nourished people in the drought by producing vegetation from her body (Kumar p. 8). Both epics and purāṇas describe Dēvi as Prakṛiti the matrix of creation. Thus Annapūraṇā is the physical and symbolical form of Absolute prakṛiti.

Why is deification or spiritual significance given to 'Anna' (food) in Hinduism? The ancient texts state that the food is called Annaṁ since it is eaten by all creatures and it eats all creatures. All creatures and purusa are produced from the essence of food; are sustained by food; and again pass into food. It is the oldest of all forms "Annaṁ hibutane jyēstam" and also the healing herb of all creatures (Ôṣādhôyyadānnaṁ). All those who worship food as Brahman obtain all food (Sarva vai tēsānnavaphu-vantiyēnnām Brahama-upāsate)". How this happens? "From infinte soul sprang forth the ether, air, fire, water, earth, herbs, food, purasa and all creatures. The one who realises that Annaṁ is nothing but Brahman knows Brāhman and it is the first step in the way of knowledge. The realisation of the fact that from Annaṁ arose Jīva, (the vital air), *prāṇa, mānas, buddhi, vignāna* and *ānanda* is the highest knowledge. (*Taittiriyôpaniṣad, Bhṛguvalli* and *Ānaṁdavallī*). In other words, since Annaṁ is means for the realisation of the truth, or the *Ātmā* is realises the truth through prāṇa, bala, vignāna, the gift of food is considered as the most valuable one. Further, without Anna no life, without life, no body can exist; therefore, prāṇa is Annaṁ; Annaṁ is prāṇa; and prāṇa is ādhāra (basis) to body. The person who realises this, i.e. prāṇa, anna and *śarīra* (body) are one, realises the truth and gets every-thing. That is why śarīra is called annada; *śarīra* is ādhāra for prāṇa; annā and prāṇa are ādhāra to śarīra. The person who understands that the prāṇa and śarīra depend on Annā and these three are interdependent will get everything: sons, grandsons and cattle, Sôma, knowledge, fame, gnāna and Brahmavarchas. Thus, whoever knows all creatures are dependent on Annaṁ, which is nothing but the Brāhaman, knows the Brāhman (Annaṁ Brahmēti Vyajanēt).

As already mentioned, from Brahman comes forth Annaṁ and the Puruṣa; and Annaṁ is means to understand Brahman through *prāṇa, mānas, vignāna* and *ānanda*. How does this happen? The Āraṇyakas state that the Jīva is covered by five kôśas or sheets namely *Annaṁayakôśa, Prāṇamayakôśa, Vigynānamayakôśa* and *Ānaṅdamayakôśas* and is satisfied by means of anna in *sūkṣhma* and *sthūlakôśas;* Thus, the Brahman who is in the form of Jīva is to be worshipped by offering anna. Therefore, the śāstras say "The mouth is altar; eating of food is hôma and food is havis equal to sôma. So the food should be offered with attention and devotion; chanting mantra. The food is the means for the Ātma to be merged into Paramatma.

Then, the food is prayed "O food, be offering to the gods presiding over the prāṇa, apāna, vyāna, udāna and samāna vāyus and let my Jīva merge into Brahman. (Brahmāni ma Ātmavratathaya).

The person who thus realises the spiritual significance of Annaṁ and identifies the Brahman ensheeted within five layers of the body which sustains the body and helps to carry the life and worldly process, is the best person. He will be bestowed with happiness, fame and all requirements in life.

That is why the offering of Anna to others is highly praised in Hinduism. Several vratas related to Annaṁ are also prescribed in the scriptures. The Ṛgveda refers to the gift of food. The *Chāndôgya upaniṣad* praises the offering of food for all creatures of all quarters, on all times. In later days this belief specifically in Buddhist inscriptions could be found. The *Taittirīya upaniṣad,* in Bhṛiguvalli refers to "Annabrahmôpāsaka vrata" . It is stated that annaṁ should not be neglected. (Annaṁ na parikshita tadvratam); annaṁ should not be abused (annaṁ na nindyat). One should make efforts to get more food to offer to the guests and the guest should not be insulted. (Annaṁbahukurvīta tadvratam and na kanchana vasatau pratyachakshata tadvratam).

The texts state that one who offers food to a annarti immediately will get food easily from his childhood. The one who offers food with hesitation will get food from his middle age and the one who offers food with hatred will get food with great difficulty in the next birth.

The *Viṣṇu dharmôttara sūtras* state that he who does not offer food willl incur sin. The purāṇas state that Annadāna is the best of all dānas. The *Agni purāṇa, Padma purāṇa, Kurma purāṇa, Nandi purāṇa* and *Vāyu purāṇas* give the benefits of *annadāna.* That is why annadāna is one of the five Mahayagnās which are to be performed everyday by house holder in ancient India. Even the sin of *brahmahatyā* can be wiped off by annadāna. It is stated that there was no equal gift to Annadāna nor is or will be (annadānāt para dānamnabhūtāni nabhaviṣyati).

The Anna which is the main source of the life is called Annapūraṇā the goddess of nourishment in the epics, purāṇas and religious literature of later period in India.

The stôtras on Annapūrṇā are mostly found in the Āgamas, Rudrayāmala, Śivarahasya, Annapūranāmantrastava, Mahā Tripurasiddhāṅta, Annapūraṇā kavacha, Annapūrṇāhavamti, Annapūrṇāmālinīnakṣatramālika (Tantrasāra) and in Bhairvahayatantra. The bījakṣaras of Annapūrṇā are *'om' 'hrīm'* and *'srīm'*, which are used in the worship of Rajarājēśwari or Lalita. Thus highest position is given to Annapūrṇā in the medieval period.

Annapūrṇā is praised as Viśālākshī (Aijananī viśālākshyānnapūrṇedayālô); Viśvaśakti, Saraswatī, Viśvamātā,

Sristịhetukavardhanī, Bhuvanēśwarī, Tripurā, Jayā, Durgā, Lakṣmī, Annadā, Durbhikṣahnāsanyā and destroyer of daridra; and prayed for welfare and food for all. "Bhavatu bhūmi subhikṣham "dhānyavittôdpanktpam" "Annadān-aniratam "dugdhānna-pūrnamitakarena cha ratnapātram", also prayed as "Vahati sakala jīvaka mannapūrṇām-amṛitābharita darvīmannapūrṇa karēna."

The iconography of Annapūrṇā is given in the Āgamas as a youthful goddess of red complexion having a face round like moon, three-eyes, high breasts; the left hand carrying a vessel set with rubies and containing honey, and the right hand spread, holding ladle. She is endowed with wristlet, hāras which rest gracefully on the chest. Annapūraṇā as having four hands holding pāśa and aṅkuśa in upper hands, and lower hand in Abhaya and Varada pose; and crest of moon adoring her head is also described in some texts.

Goddess Annapūrṇā is the presiding deity of Kāśī, the most sacred place of India. The vēdas, epics and jātakas refer to Kāśī as one of the important kingdom of that period. The *Kumārsambhāva of Kalidasa* (4-5 century A.D. refers to Kāśī and goddess Annapūrṇā. Dēvi Bhāgavata (3-4 century A.D.) while referring to śākta pithas describes at one point, Annapūrṇā as goddess of Kāñchipura while in another place refers Viśālākshi as the goddess of Vārānaśi which is also a śākta pīṭha.

The *Śkānda purāṇa* of *c.* 700 A.D. gives the greatness of Kāśī while narrating the story of sage Vyāsa and his curse to Kāśī for not giving him food, whereupon goddess Viśālākshī appeared as a house wife and offered food to Vyāsa. The *Lingapurāṇa* states that Śiva used to beg food and support his children; but one day, he could not get any food due to the miracle used by Śakti. Finally Śakti as Annapūrṇā offered food to Śiva at the door steps. It is believed that only Annapūraṇā could satisfy the hunger of

Kasipet

Śiva. So, in her honour, Śiva built the city Kāśī with Annapūrṇā as the main deity.

Thus, the cult goddess Annapūrṇā is as old as human race; however, very few temples are dedicated to Annapūrṇā in the country. The existing temple of Annapūrṇā at Kāśī was built (renovated) by Pēśwās of Poona in 18th century. Slowly the goddesses Viśālākshī and Annapūrṇā evolved into two separate goddesses and were worshipped in two different shrines at Kāśī.

Coming to Āndhra, greatness of the goddess of Annapūrṇā and that of Kāśī was described in *Kumārasambhāva* written by Nannechôla a śaiva poet of 12th century A.D and in Kāsikhanda by Śrīnātha a poet of 13th century A.D.

In this regard, *Śankara's Annapūrṇā stôtra* dated of 8-10 century A.D. needs special mention. All verses in his Annapūrṇā stôtra describe the goddess as holding pustaka, akṣhmāla and as opener of the doors of *Môksha*. Thus, it appear Śaṅkara prayed to Annapūraṇā not for physical nourishment but for spiritual perfection.

Though Annapūrṇā is the universal mother, only a few temples are dedicated to her, and most of them are found in South India only. In Āndhra the Śiva temples generally are called as Kāśī Viśweswara temples and the feeding houses attached to these temples as Annapūrṇā sattras. The river Gôdāvari in Telangānā region is referred to as Gangā reflecting the respect for Kāśī, Śiva, Annapūrṇā and Gangā and on account of the agrarian background of the area.

" Annapūrita hēmapātra subhaga
mannēśvarīm tvām bhaje" .

2

BRĀHMANISM UNDER THE SĀTAVĀHANAS

" Pramadhapatē rôṣāruṇa Gôwrī mukhja chandra sangna pratimām

kalitārdha sarasīruhamiva Saṅdhyā salilāñjyalīm namaḥ"

This verse invocating Śiva as Ardhanārīśvara offering Saṅdhya is composed by king Hāla, the seventeenth king of the Sātavāhana dynasty. The Sātavāhanas who ruled over Deccan for about four hundred years (2nd century B.C.—2nd century A.D.) were great patrons of Brāhmanism. King Śātakarṇi is praised as "Eka Brāhmaṇa" and "Protector of Varṇāsrama Dharma" . The kings and the people upheld *Dharma* and the donations made were called *Dharma Sētu* or *Dharma Sthāpitam*. The Nānāghāt, Nāsik and Tālguṅḍa inscriptions issued by the kings of this dynasty show that Vēdism, Śaivism, Bhāghavatism and other Brāhmanical cults and traditions flourished during their period. The archaeological finds and the literary sources Gāhāsaptaśathi testifies this view. While the former reveals mainly the court religion, the latter popular faith.

The Nānāghat inscription issued by Queen Nāyanikā (2nd B.C.) gives the list of innumerable sacrifices like Agnādhaya, Agnihôtra, Apratyôma, Atirātra, Gargyātri-ratra, Sabalihôma, Gôsava, Rājasūya and Aśvamēdh, etc.

performed by the king or the Queen on his behalf and to the lavish *dakṣhiṇās* given to the priests and to the Sadas on these occasions. The name of the king "Yajñaśrī" further testifies devotion to Vēdism. Yajñaśālā and the sacrifical animal are referred to in the Gādhāsaptaśathi. Brāhmanical faiths, beliefs and practices that were prevalent during the Sātavāhana period are narrated below.

Śaivism

Rudra-śiva who is called Paśupati, Saṁbhu, Pramadhādhipa too in the vedic period; around whom innumerable stories were woven in the epics and purāṇas was installed and whorshipped at Guḍimallam in Chittoor district (2nd B.C.) probably in the time of the Sātavāhanas. The Cave at Naśik donated by the Queen to the Buddhists was compared to Kailasa, the abode of Śiva known for its beauty and loftiness. The Caturmukha Liṅga from Amaravati now kept in the State Museum indicates that Pāśupata cult of Śaivism was also practised in those days.

King Hāla praised and worshipped Śiva as Ardhanārīśvara; and Śiva and Pārvatī as an ideal couple, who are always ready to listen to the prayers of the devotees, protect and bestow booms. The names like Iśvara, Paramēśvara, Śēkhara, Śivapalita. Riṣabha Datta, Śiva Datta, Bhūtapāla, Bhavasôpa point out the popularity of Śiva. The Kāpālika sect of Śaivism also was followed in that period. An inscription of Śātavāhanas from Tāligunḍa reveals that Śiva adorned with matted hair was worshipped in the form of eternal sthanu. The names of the poets Śivaskandita, Skandapālita, show that the cult of Skanda was also practised.

Vaishnavism

God Viṣṇu who is identified with Bhaga and Sūrya in the Vēda; With Nārāyaṇa and Hari in the Brāhmaṇas; and with Kriṣṇa son of Yasôda in the Upaniṣads, Epics and Purāṇās was popular in the times of Śatavahānas. The avatāras, assumed by Viṣṇu to subdue the evil were popular during the period.

The Nānāghat and Nāśik inscriptions of early Sātavāhanas refer to Vāsudēva-Saṅkarṣaṇa; Rāma and Kēśava respectively. Names like Gôvardhana and Sudarśana which are connected with Viṣṇu cult are also referred to in the records of the period. The story of churning of Milk Ocean with Mēruparvata by using serpent Anaṅta as rope by the Gods; birth/origin of several precious gems and *Amṛita* in the course of churning was very famous among the folk. The Viṅdhya mountains covered with row of clouds are compared to Lord Viṣṇu whose body is bathed in spray of Ocean of milk. Nārāyaṇa adorned with Koustubha along with his spouse Lakṣmī was prayed by King Hāla. The Vāmanāvatara which was taken up by Hari to subdue Bali, demanding only three feet of land was also highly praised by the folk. The stories of Yasôda's meternal affections, Gôpikā's love for Kriṣṇa, their secret affairs, scoldings, Kriṣṇa's special liking for Rādhā, his support to Bhīma while killing Duryôdhana were popular during the period. A Gôpikā is described as kissing the reflection of Kriṣṇa on a cheek of another Gôpikā with the pretext of praising her dance. This recalls the description of Rāsalīlā or Kaumudī Utṣava where the Gôpikās formed a circle with Kriṣṇa in between and danced.

"Rāsôstvaḥd Saṁprāvro Gôpī maṅḍala maṅḍitaḥ
Yôgēśwarēṇa Kṛiṣṇē tāsāṁ madhyēdvayôrdhvaôḥ
Praviṣṭēna gṛihītānāṁ kaṇṭhē svanikaṭaṁ sthriyah"

(Bhāgavata. X)

The name of the king as Kriṣṇa, the names used for referring Kriṣṇa such as Dāmôdara, Madhumadana, Hari, Nārāyaṇa, Trivikrama and Madhūsudana testify the various aspects of the religious sect known in those days.

Worship of other gods

The Vēdas and Sūtras considered Gaṇapati as the god who

causes obstacles, however as one, who causes success when appeased by offering certain rites outside the village. The figures of Gaṇapati found at Koṅḍapur and Amarāvati assigned to 1st to 2nd century B.C also reflect the practice of Gaṇapati cult in Āndhra. The name of the Sātavāhana king Lambôdara and the three verses from Gāthasaptaśathi, which describes the idol of Vināyaka kept in secluded place, and ferocious act of the deity show that Ganapati too was worshipped during the Sātavāhanas.

The adoration to Sūrya, Chandra, Indra, Vāsava, Yama, Varuna, Kubēra along with Dikpālas is found in the Nānāghāt inscription of Sātavāhanas. The earliest figures of Sūrya and Indra were sculptured in caves of Bhāja (2nd B.C.) also belong to same dynasty. Sūrya was worshipped by sipping water and uttering Gāyatrimantra. The deity was described as travelling in chariot; as an ornament to the sky and as source of happiness to all. The birth of Chandra from the ocean of milk and his enemity with Rāhu was well known to the foḷk. The Moon was worshipped both by men and women by offering flowers. Manmatha, the God of love is described as active with flower arrows and bows, dwelling in bowers. Brahmā as the creator and Agni as fond of women as described in epics and purāṇas was popular in days of Sātavāhanas.

The earliest form of Lakṣmī in India is stated to be found at Amarāvati represented as a Lady sitting on lotus and also in the form of Śrīvasta. The excavation conducted at Peddabankur in Āndhra Pradesh revealed still earlier form of this goddess, standing, being bathed by the two elephants as described in the Śrīsūkta of Ṛgvēda. The Birth of Lakṣmī from milk ocean was highly euologied, and every auspicious sign, victory and happy affairs is attributed to her in the form of Śrī. The Gāthāsaptaśatī describes a lady pounding rice, with the flour spread and sprinkled all over the body as Dēvī Lakṣmī rising from Milk Ocean.

Mother Goddess is worshipped in various forms during

this period as revealed by the excavation conducted at Peddabaṇkur, Koṅḍapūr, Dhūlikatta and other Śatavāhana sites in Āndhra Pradesh. Every village has a temple for Goddess. The terms such as Pārvatī, Gowrī, Āryā, show that the benegnant as well as ferocious aspects of Gowrī were worshipped. Dedication of bells in the temple of Chaṅḍikā was in practice. Outside the village, temples for the tutelary deites were constructed. High position is given to Bhūdēvī (Aditi) as in the Vēdas. She is shown in the art of Amarāvatī also, as witnessing a great deed.

The ethical ideals of *Rāmāyaṇa* were highly valued and practised in the times of the Sātavāhanas.

Demi-god Yakṣha in the early period, was worshipped along with other gods. But afterwords Yakṣha was worshipped in association with trees. The Yakṣhas, both as handsome and young; dwarf and ferocious are depicted at Amarāvatī. The excavation at Dhūlikatta and other sites brought to light the figures of Yaksha. The description that king Sātakarṇi was helped by the Gandharvas in his battle shows that the tradition that Gandharvas are the divine fighters was popular in the Sātavāhana times. The Apsaras and Vidyādharas who are praised for their beauty; and the Siddhas, Caraṇas, Sādhyās and other demi-gods were popular among the folk. The Garuḍa, Nāga and Kinnaras were the other group of semi-divine beings who were frequently sculptured in the art of Sātavāhanas. The nāgas are considered as the guardians of hidden treasure too. Thus, the Brāhmanical mythology which extended from the celestral trees, animals, Nandanavanas, Kalpataru to various lôkas; and demi-gods and Rishis were sculptured at Bhāja, Kārle and Amarāvatī under the Sātavāhana rule.

The River Goddess Gaṅgā seated on her crocodile vehicle; and as carrying food and water was depicted at Amarāvati and this is the first representation of river goddess in India.

The commonners believed that trees are endowed with life spirit; so, the trees were depicted in art as *vanadēvtās* by representing as having head or hand at times.

Legendary Figures

The great kings Nahuṣa, Nābhāga, Janamējaya, Sagara, Yayāti, Aṁbariṣa were taken as ideal by king Goutamīputra Sātakarṇi. Divine rishis were also taken as ideal for their spiritual and virtuous life.

Mythical animals

Various types of hybrid animals sculptured at Amarā-vatī reflect the fancy and imagination of the people about the biological evolution.

Other Practices

Satī was practised in those days quite willingly by women wearing particular type of dress and ornaments; forced satī also was in practice. Since polygamy was in practice, all the wives used to become satīs at times. However, even women used to participate in cremation and other burial rites. The worship of the dead was also in practice by erecting memorials depicting the figure of hero in honour of which the memorial was raised.

People led the life according to the rules ordained by the Saṁhitās and Smṛitis. Every householder used to offer Gāyatrī even in dead winter. Gods were consecrated and worshipped by offering water and flowers. Charity was considered as virtue and the kāka bali was performed by householders. In the absence of the householder, his wife used to perform the rite. Women used to lead life according to Dharmaśāstras; they worshipped husband, by washing his feet twice in a day and used to worship the elder members like mother-in-law.

Vratas

Queeṅ Nāyanikā was highly praised for performing

māsôpavāsa and dīrghavratas and other ascetic rites. Queen Bālaśrī lead life like Royal Rishis wife even at home. Women, in Sātavāhana period believed that they can obtain worthy and desired husband by doing vratas (accumulation of past good deeds) and by dying with the same desire. The Shyāmaśabala vrata was performed by women for self-purification by entering first fire and then water. At the end of the observance of a vrata, women used to distribute vāyanas in the village going from house to house. Even Vaiśya women used to do vratas and distribute vāyanas of sweet meats in the village going from house to house; even to the people of other castes. In the beginning of the rainy season (before beginning the agricultural work) in the fields, plough was worshipped for good rain and crop; it may be the Sītayagna prescribed in Sūtras. Lotus flowers placed on a pūrṇakumbha was an important object of reverence in those days.

Festivals

The inscriptions refer to festival, in general without mentioning any specific name. The Gāthāśaptasatī on the other hand refers to the festivals which have no religious bearing; but were intended to enjoy life and the beauty of season. On a festival day, women used to take bath in congregation, a special bath, and prepare delicious dishes. All people congregate in a special area and play drums and pipes. When the festivity was over the idol worshipped was taken in procession to the outskirts of the village. On the day of Phālgunôtsava or Madanôtsava, men and women used to wear new red clothes; flowers as ornaments; enjoy drinks and spray or sprinkle coloured powder on each other irrespective of sex.

People in those days, were influenced by charms. The practice of spell for the bite of scorpion, to drive devil and the belief that the hidden treasure being guarded by the Nāgas was described in Gāthāsaptaśatī.

People considered Pūrṇakalasa with fresh leaves, mango flower and lotus flower, as auspicious; may be on this account, the whole Art of Sātavāhanas was profusely decorated with Pūrṇakalasas, garlands, lotus etc. The Pūrṇakalaśa was used at the time of welcoming as well as seeing off dear and near. Similarly, flower garland was hung on the threshold as a symbol of welcome. Before commencing any writing, swastika, the auspicious sign was used. The throbbing of left eye was considered as good omen for ladies. It was a custom to find some auspicious hour to commence their journey by calculating the favourable planetary position. The folk never moved out of the house on Maṅgalwar and in guru dôṣa and when animal krisṇasāra passed from right side to left.

People believed in the polytheism, heaven, hell, merit, other worlds, sin, rebirth, fate, perishability of life, authority of the smritis, curse, śapatha (oath taking) and prāyaśchitta. In those days folk believed that whatever one desired would be obtained in next birth; in the niṣkāmakarma (to do one's duty without aspiring for fruits); soul as witness of one's deeds; and death on the banks of river Tapati as meritorious. These are some of the popular believes of the Sātavāhana period.

Though, so far, we have not come across any remains of the Sātavāhana temple of early period, The Gāthāsaptaśatī describes a ruined temple and the gatherings of pigeons around the śūla (rod) . We come to know that temples were used as rest houses, auditoriums for cultural programmes and for secret meetings too.

Thus, it is clear that Brāhmanism with its imaginatively and thickly woven network embraced the life of Sātavāhana period, though Buddhism was adopted by a group of people as a fashion of the day. The inherent and native cults, beliefs and practices never could be forgotten by people, though Buddhism was adopted. Not only then, even today, it is the same case. Some of the practices which were followed by the people of Sātavāhana times, still continue and are followed in the interior villages, i.e. the excavations at Peddabankur in Karimnagar district of Āndhra Pradesh brought to light a pot stampped with 3 leaves, kept on a platform which has been interpreted as an object of venertion. The same practice is followed even today. In the houses of the farmers, in Karimnagar district, a pot called *kalikuṅḍa* is kept in a specific place and filled with water and food and is prayed with reverence.

The Gāthāsaptaśatī is one of the muktakāvyas in prākṛit language, consisting of 700 errotic verses composed by different writers including some poetesses. It was compiled by king Hāla, the 11th king of the Sātavāhana dynasty.

The above study of the different religious beliefs as gathered from in Gāthāsaptaśati, reveals that the Śaivism, Bhāgavatism, and other cults were popular among rural life of ancient Āndhra and the village folk was free from the domination of the priest craft, complicated rituals; and their way of worship was very simple. Neither, the complicated rituals and priest craft could influence them nor dry and strict ethical code of Buddhism could inculcate human feelings in them and could satisfy their emotional yearning like the Hindu mythology with its huge and thrilling pantheon. As such, they preferred and wanted a warm-worship, consoling grace, which can lessen the gulf between humanself and the supreme soul. Thus the path of Bhakti took the higher place in the hearts of village people, than Vēdism and Buddhism.

The religion of early Āndhra as understood from the Gāthāsaptaśatī is totally different from that we understand from epigraphical, archaeological and numesmatic study. But in no way, it in an antagonism to the latter, but only an addition to it, Thus giving a bright colour and wholeness to Hinduism and to the religion of Ancient Āndhra.

Though so far, we do not have any direct evidence such as inscriptions proclaiming the valour of king Hāla, he handed over to us the Gāthāsaptaśatī revealing his unfathomble admiration for prākrit language and his poetic skill. We still cherish Hāla in our minds for giving us a recorded work of that period. The Gāthāsaptaśatī and Āndhras are indebted to Hāla.

(This article was read in Sātavāhana seminar held at Hyderabad in 1981.)

Books referred

1. *Gāthāsaptaśatesāramu*–Rallapalli Ananta Krishna Sarma.
2. *Gāthāsaptaśatī*–Gatti Lakṣmī Narasimha Sastry
3. *Gāthāsaptaśatīsaramu*–Kuchibhottla Prabhakara-swamy veeraraghavaswamy
4. *Saṁskṛuta Gāthāsaptaśatī*–Madhuranadha Sastry.
5. *Hindigāthāsaptasatī*–Narmadeswar Chaturvedi.
6. *Saptaśatīsarm* (Pedakamativema) – D.V. Sītaramaswamy.
7. *Early Āndhra Iconography and Scultures* by Dr. C Śiva Ramamurti.
8. *Epigraphia Indica* Vol. VIII and XVIII.
9. *Archaeological Survey of Western India* Vol. V, XV.
10. *Elements of Iconography*–by Sri Gopinath Rao Vol.II.
11. *Art of Amaravati*–AP Archaeological Series No. 57.

References

Subject	V.No in Gāthāsaptaśatī
Heaven	1.75, 2.25
Merit	6.75, 5.62, 2.74, 2.78, 1.99
Charity according to rules	1.68, 3.
Śapatha	4.57, 5.48 (Kôśapana)
Curse	
Dharma	6.14, 3.79
Hrudayame Sākśhī	3.1
whatever we desire, we get	4.75
Vidyādharī	5.46
Sarparakshitanidhi	6.76

Śaivism	1.1, 1.69, 5.8, 5.48, 5.55, 5.67, 7.100
Vaiṣnavism	1.89, 2.12, 2.14, 2.17, 2.51, 5.5, 5.6, 5.11 5.25 5.43, 5.48, 7.55, 7.69
Buddhism	2.62, 2.67, 2.75, 4.8, 6.53.
Vināyaka	4.72, 5.3
Sūrya	1.34, 4.32, 7.53, 1.1, 5.48, 7.100, 4.30
Chandra	1.16, 4.19, 7.57, 4.46, 2.51
Agni	1.14, 3.11
Indra	?
Yagna	3.27
Rāmāyaṇa	1.35, 4.11
Mahābhārata	5.43
Satī	5.7, 7.33, 5.49, 2.4
Temple	1.64, 2.9, 2.72, 2.90, 2.94, 2.76, 4.32
Brahmā	3.7
Manmatha	2.47, 2.77, 3.10, 4.24, 25, 4.26, 4.71, 5.41, 5.59, 5.73, 6.20 etc.
Vasanta	2.28
Samudramanthana	5.75, 6.93
Daily duties	2.30, 3.5, 4.30, 4.55, 5.93, 2.62
Auspicious and	1.25, 2.37, 3.14
unauspicious signs	3.44, 56, 61, 62, 4.38, 46, 4.38, 7.42, 7.6
Charms	3.37
Festivals	1.79, 2.94, 4.12, 4.69, 5.34, 6.44, 4.45, 7.24
Worship	4.38, 7.6
Prāyaśchitta	5.48
Vratas	1.99, 2.85, 3.11, 4.28, 7.3, 2.19, 20
Gods & Nymphs	2.76, 5.46, 6.92, 9.3, 1.42
Belief in other worlds	7.8, 7.31, 7.56, 3.7
	2.83, 3.67
Rebirth	5.41, 4.75, 7.8
Fruits left to god (fate)	3.79
Fate	3.4, 3.45, 2.32, 3.79, 7.56
Perishability of life	3.47, 5.86
Bhūdēvi	5.34
Eclipse	4.19

3

FLORA AND FAUNA IN ANCIENT ĀNDHRA

The plant and animal kingdoms are the first living creatures on the earth from which human race evolved. Being the main source of sustenance for man the flora and fauna have great impact on human life.

Ancient Āndhra Dēśa was bounded by Sea on East, Vindhyas on North; Sahyadri on West; Nallamalai on South which also help in water shedding the mighty rivers like Krishna, Godavari, Tapati and like, besides many other rivulet and the deltas where these rivers fall into the sea. Thus the soil of the area is very fertile and conducive for the growth and production of variety of cereals, pulses, different types of fruit bearing trees, shrubs, bowers, creepers and a variety of fauna. Since prehistoric time, this fertile land promoted the growth of healthy and beautiful bio-sphere.

The flora promoted a good aestheic environment and the products which had economic, cosmetic and medicinal value while the fauna helped in the development of economic and nutritious food material for the inhabitants. The Sātavāhanas who held sway from the eastern ocean to the western ocean promoted trade which had knots with the flora and fauna flourished in their kingdom. The

Gādhāsaptaśati a muktakāvya compiled by king Hāla consisting of 700 verses composed by various poets and poetesses gives a picturesque description of contemporary flora and fauna and village life of Sātavāhana period.

The flora is classified into trees, herbs, shurbs, creepers and acquatic plants in general terms. Their collective place is called a forest or farm or field. The thick forests, forest-fire, forest villages and green grassfields are frequently referred to in Gāthāsaptaśatī. The villages were surrounded by agricultural lands. The fields were ploughed in rainy season, seeds were sown; after the crop had grown well, paddy was reaped in winter season. A variety of paddy were grown. Besides cotton, turmeric, hemp, redgram, gingely were cultivated. The peanut, gram, sugarcane, mustard, castor, and great millet were also grown. The frequently mentioned tree that produced edible fruits is mango. The elephant apple, rose apple, cucumber, jack fruit were also available in plenty.

The saffron, camphor, sandal wood and soapnut were the cosmetic raw materials that were referred to in Gādhāsaptaśatī. The sandal paste was applied to the body in the summer to cool the body and also as tilaka on the forehead. Scents of roses were also used. The lac was applied on the feet for the beautification. The camphor was used probably for eyes. The other trees which have aromatic value, medicinal value and helped in developing the healthy environment are the margosa, sāl, vaṭ, śirīṣa, vakula, punnāga, mālatī, kadamba, madhūka, aśôka, palāśa, pāṭala, dāsāni, sēfālikā, kuṁda, tilaka, kuravaka, virajāji, guṁja, pārijāta, silk cotton, and goldmohar. The bamboo and the elephant grass might have been used for construction purposes.

The rose apple leaves, kadaṁaba flowers, black lotus were applied on the ear as the decoration. The ripe palm leaves are also used as an object of ornamentation. The flowers of kadaṁba, raktapātala, dāsāni, black lotus were also used for their sweet smell besides madhūka, kuruvaka and aśôka. The flowering creepers are planted around the stepped well. The lotus and lily ponds are frequently mentioned and the lotus flower or petals are always compared to beautiful face or eyes of the ladies while, the leg of women is compared to the plantain tree. The delicate organs of the rural lady are campared to śhirīṣa flower.

Among the acquatic plants, many types of bulbs are referred to. The red lotus, white lotus, blue lotus, kāsa and white lilies are frequently described.

The relics of vēdic idea attributing divinity to nature or worshipping nature as God is found in Gāthāsaptaśati. Every village had a banayan tree in the centre which is worshipped and in the outskirts of the village, idol of Gaṇapati is placed under a tree. The red flowers shed on the ground are compared to the Buddhist Bhikshu, wearing orange robes, prostrated before Lord Buddha.

The fauna mentioned in the Gāthāsaptaśatī is also of wide spectrum. Both vertebrates, invertebrates; like reptiles, aves, orthropodes and mammalia are mentioned. All types of animals were described in the most naturalistic manner.

Among the aquatic animals shells, coral, fish, tortoise and frog are found mentioned. The python, cobra, scorpion, bees, spiders, nimbakīṭa, gingari, shining creatures and mosquitoes are some of the orthopodes mentioned.

Among birds, peacock is the most referred to besides, parrot and maina. The swan, dove, crow, hen, crane and other water birds are also described in the Gādhāsaptaśatī.

The mammalia comprise the major portion of the fauna, as the villages were surrounded with thick forests and big trees. While the cow, buffallow and calf, the main means of agricultural activities are frequently referred to the dog, pig, monkey, lion, boar and cat are described in their natural habitat.

While describing hot-summer, it is stated that when the whole water of a tank dried up the fish, shells and tortoise died on the tank-bed only are seen. Further, the slough of the cobra hanging from the boulders was described as being licked by the wild buffallow mistaking it for water-fall. In another verse, the serpent is described as guarding the hidden treasure.

The swarms of bees and their humming, hoaring around flower bunches is described in several verses. Also the sound of other orthropods, like chimmata, humming creature was described in several verses. In a verse, spider hanging ups and down along with its web is compared to a vakula flower. Yet in another verse, the sound of mosquito is compared to the melody of vīṇā.

The peacock with spreading blue neck for drinking rain drops, it's colourful feathers and its dance during rainy season are described in Gādhāsaptaśatī beautifully. The rows of parrots flying in the sky are compared to emerlads in the necklace of goddess of the sky. Generally, the parrots are pet birds and kept in the cages by the young damsels. Maina is another bird which is kept in cages and used to converse.

As it is well known, dove is considered as bird symbol of conjugal love. Swan, the sacred bird is praised for its capacity to separate water from milk. Another water bird, crane, seated on a lotus leave is compared to śaṅkh kept on a green plate in one verse.

Groups of crows, crow-nest, crow eating fruits, and bali offered by women; and cry of crow as symbol of early morning are described in typical ethnic and natural way.

Since Āndhra is basically an agricultural land, milch cow, oxen, calf and cow pen are described in many verses, as well the buffallow are described in nearly ten verses.

The thick forests near the villages were the habitant of

deers and elephants. The deer is praised for its beautiful eyes, conjugal love, innocence and pitied for suffering from forest-fire. The spotted deer, black buck and deer are referred to. The elephants enjoying the bath in the lotus tanks, their sweat, pearls from their head and their romance are described in a dozen verses. The lion, boar, wild pig and the other forest animals are described with reference to their destructive activities of agriculture and such.

The cat eating ghee and milk; monkey eating a blackbee mistaking it for a rose apple and the domestic dog guarding the village and house are described in typical rural style.

That was the ecology of Anciant Andhra Desa.

(Paper was read in Indian History Congress held at Hyderabad in 1982.)

References

	Name of Flora	Verse Nos in Gāthāśapthaśati
1.	Mango (*Mangifera indica*)	1.19, 7.66, 1.62, 4.31, 2.43, 4.96, 5.99, 6.42, 6.75, 6.95, 1.19, 1.97
2.	Elephant apple (*Limoniaci dissina*)	30.6, 7.41
3.	Margosa (*Azadirachta indica*)	2.48, 3.47
4.	Pīpal (*Ficus glomerata*)	
5.	Sāl (*Slorea robusta*)	In Art
6.	Banayan (*Ficus bengalensis linn*)	2.66, 2.67, 3.94, 6.56, 1.94, 2.21
7.	Rose apple (*Syzgium jambos*)	2.80, 5.19, 6.3, 2.40, 2.93
8.	Soapnut (*Sapindas mukorossi*)	2.89
9.	Palmtree (*Borassw flabellifer*)	4.98
10.	Lotus (*Nelumbium speicosum*)	14.11, 1.8, 7.41, 1.78, 2.10, 2.87, 5.34, 5.26, 4.43, 5.94, 7.22, 2.88, 7.24, 7.19, 1.5, 2.6, 2.32, 2.76
11.	Berry (*Flacourtia ramontchi*)	?
12.	Lilly (*Nymphaeonioh*)	54.37, 15, 56, 2, 88, 4.23, 5.36
13.	Śirīṣa (*Albizzialebbok*)	2.45, 1.55, 2.25
14.	Vakula (*Minusophb elenglinne*)	1.63

15. Mālatā (*Jasmimumgrondi flur*)	1.9, 1.82, 2.59, 5.26, 5.42, 5.44
16. Kadamba (*Anthocephalus cadamba*)	1.37, 2.77, 4.14, 6.64, 6.65, 7.36
17. Madhūka (*Passia latifolia*)	2.4, 2.3, 2.59
18. Aśôka (*Saraca indica*)	2.79, 1.7, 5.4
19. Palāśa (*Butea monosperme*)	2.79, 4.8, 4.11
20. Dāsāni (*Hibiscus*)	2.45
21. Pātala	5.69, 1.14
22. Śēphalika	5.12
23. Kundatilaka	2.87, 6.91, 6.90, 5.26
24. Kuravaka (*Polanisiacosmdee Blrleriaprionitis*)	1.6, 3.19
25. Bamboo (*Bambusa tulda*)	1.80, 7.74, 7.35
26. Banana (*Musa Paradisaca*)	1.52
27. Castor(*Picins commus*)	3.57
28. Virajaji (*Prosopus spicigre*)	4.22
29. Nettle (*Edipto heyne or Tragiain voluerata*)	6.32
30. Guṅja (*Abruspreatorius*)	4.10
31. Paddy (*Oryzasatira*)	1.9, 5.2, 6.62, 6.49, 6.68, 67, 7.90, 7.89, 7.92, 7.91
32. Cotton (*Cossypium herbaceum*)	2.65, 4.59, 6.49, 4.60
33. Sugarcane (*Saccharum officinarum*)	6.41, 6.54
34. Gram (*Cerar ertenum*)	6.57
35. Cucumber (*Cucumis sativas*)	6.34
36. Elephant Grass	5.34
37. Pigeon Pea (*Cajamuscajam*)	4.58
38. Coccinia cordifolia	7.41
39. Indianhemp (*Crotalaria juncia*)	1.9
40. Turmeric (*Curcuma domistica*)	1.58, 3.46
41. Dog Grass (*Orsedge cyndondactylon*)	5.34
42. Camphor (*Cmnamonun connphora*)	1.32
43. Saffron (*Crocus satvia*)	2.98, 2.69
44. Sandal Wood (*Santal umobun*)	1.16, 3.88
45 Night Jasmine (*Nyctanthesarb or Histes*)	In Art
46. Madhavi (*Hiptage madablote*)	4.22
47. Gingelly (*Sesanum zondia*)	1.8, 7.27, 7.93

48. Mustard	2.71
49. Maruvaka	7.77
50. Lac	2.27, 7.4
51. Draks	3.69
52. Kusumbha	4.92
53. Ankota	4.13
54. Sāl	4.16
55. Palm	4.98
56. Viṣakandalika	5.10
57. Vanjula	5.22

Name of Fauna			*V.No.in Gathasaptasatī*
Mammalia			
1. Lion		-	275
2. Elephant		-	2.21, 2.73, 2.58, 3.58, Romance 4.73, 7.30, 5.54, Elephant Pearls,7.40
3. Horse	-	Coinage of Sātavāhanas	-
4. Bull & Calf	-	-	1.19, 1.65, 7.92, 2.5, 5.60, 3.38, 3.75, 5.47, 7.38
5. Deer	-	-	2.87, 6.88, 6.94, 1.25
Deerskin	-	-	7.29
F.Deer	-	-	7.1, 7.18
6. Boachs	-	-	5.2 ?
7. Cow	- Herd	-	5.47, 7.37, 38, 3.71, 7.9, 7.98
8. Buffalo	-	-	2.71, 2.72, 5.96, 6.49, 6.51, 7.80, 1.65, 6.3, 6.10, 6.60, 6.74, 6.84
9. Monkey	-	-	6.31, 6.32
10. Ass	- Ar.W.I.	-	
11. Dog	-	-	7.62, 7.88, 2.75, 2.38, 7.86, 87, 88, 6.49, 57, 62, 7.87, 7.88
12. Cat	-	-	2.86, 3.63
13. Bear		-	2.9
13a. Boar	-	-	3.2
Raptiles			
14. a) Snake	-	-	6.51
b) Panther	-	-	7.40

Aves

15. Swan	-	-	2.10, 7.24, 7.76
16. Crane	-	-	1.4, 1.78, 7.60
17. Crow	-	-	2.2, 2.92, 3.5, 3.47, 5.35, 3.48, 6.63, 6.92 6.72, 7.98, 7.82
18. Parrot	-	-	1.75, 2.63, 3.8, 6.63, 7.66, 6.62, 6.78, 4.38, 4.8, 6.51, 6.89
19. Maina	-	-	2.20, 2.64, 6.78, 6.50, 3.20
20. Peacock	-	-	5.4, 2.74, 4.94, 7.36, 1.52, 6.59
21. Dove	-	-	1.64

Arthropodes

22. Spider	-	-	1.63
23. Mosquitoes	-	-	6.60
24. Ksinchurai	- Gingari	-	5.94
25. Bees	-	-	1.37, 1.92, 2.28, 2.39, 1.78, 4.87, 5.58
26. Scorpion	-	-	3.37

Aquatic animals

27. Crab	-	-	1.9, 5.14
28. Śankh	-	-	1.4
29. Frog	-	-	4.91
30. Pearl Oyster	-	-	4.10
31. Fish	-	-	5.14
32. Tortoise	-	-	5.14
33. Coral	-	-	7.78
34. Water bird	-	-	7.60

4

GUḌIMALLAM-ŚIVA?

Guḍimallam (lat. $13^{o}.35N$ and long. $79^{o}.34E$) is a village located 21 kilometers to the south-west of Kāḷahasti (Lat. $13^{o}.45N$ long. 79.45E) a famous Saiva centre in Śrīkālahasti taluk, Chittoor distt. of Āndhra Pradesh. River Swarṇa-mukhi flows one kilometer north-west of this village.

The environ of Guḍimallam village has distant hills of trapezoid rock called Tirupati Khandolite, hill forest area of Tirumula and Horsely hills. These hills, plains and valley make this area picturesque. The eastern ghat passess through Kālahasti and entres Kuppam. The river Swarnamukhi which rises in Chandragiri hills passes through valley reaches Kālahasti, then flows to Nellor and joins sea at Gūḍūru. At Kālahasti, another riverlet Kalyna joins Swarnamukhi. The area has been in habited by several tribes like souras, kôyas, sugālis, cheṅchus, kuruas and other types.[1]

The Parasurāmēśvara temple of Guḍimallam is gajapriṣta type, bearing epigraphical evidence from 7th century A.D. to 18th century A.D. The excavations undertaken by Dr. I.K. Sarma, from Archaeological Survey of India revealed that in phase I śilāprākāra of *liṅga* was set up in second century B.C. and that in phase II the apsidal temple in brick was raised during second-third century A.D. The practice of worship of *liṅga*-in-railing

The Liṅga

under the trees or over a pedestal in the open belongs to third century B.C. as found at Mathura, and coins motif from Taxila and Ujjain datable to 3rd to 2nd century B.C. Such practice was mentioned by Aśôka in Rummindei pillar inscription as Śivasthala. The Vēdas refer such practice as Yakshasadanam.

The Parasūrāmēśvara *liṅga* at Guḍimallam is made out of reddish ignious rock available in the hill range of Tirupati, Distt. Chitoor , Āndhra Pradesh. Dr. I.K. Sharma observed that "The *Liṅga* is set directly on the floor of the central shrine and the pindika or the pedestal is cut out in the form of a quadrangular ridge on the ground; the *liṅga* is exactly five feet in height and bears upon its front portion a beautiful figure of Śiva.[2]

The figure of *liṅga* has two arms, in the right one of which a ram is held by its hind legs and with its head hanging downwards, in the left one is held a water-pot, and a battle-axe (*paraśu*) rests upon the left shoulder. "On the head of the figure is a covering, resembling a turban, of plaited, not matted, hair. The face is distinctly Mongoloid in its features with oblique eyes'. 'There are *kuṅḍalas* in the ears, the lobes of which are distended so as to hang down as far as the shoulders; on each of the upper-arms is a highly finished ornamental band (aṅgada) and on the forearms five bracelets of different patterns. Round the neck is to be seen a necklace of rare workmanship, it is noteworthy that there is no yājnôpavīta, the Brāhmanical sacred thread. The image wears cloth on loin (like *dhoti*)".

'The figure of Śiva stands astride upon the shoulders of a Rākṣasa, the Apasmāra puruṣa, who is sitting on the ground on his haunches and supporting himself with his hands which are planted on the ground near the feet. He too has a sort of jaṭāmakuṭa on his head and a hāra of beads round his neck. He is swathy and burly in the build of his body, possesses a pair of pointed animal ears and is, withal, jolly and happy as is evidenced from the broad grin on his face'.[3]

This unique *liṅga*, from Guḍimallam bearing a standing figure is a class itself. The figure has been identified by scholars as noted below.

Shri Gopinath Rao assigned the *liṅga* on stylistic grounds to first or 2nd century B.C. Shri Nilakantha Shastri concedes that this monumental *liṅga* is quite out of the way and it is difficult to find its place in the evolution of South Indian iconography. Smt. Stella Kramrish dated it to first century B.C. Shri Śivaramamurti categorically states that it is a unique piece of early Sātavāhana art from its close affinity to Bharhut Yakṣhas. Shri Bhandarkar thought that it belongs to Gupta period and assigned to the fourth century A.D. Shri Soundara Rajan regarded the *liṅga* as of Lakulisa sect and assigned to sixth-seventh century A.D., Shri Ananda Coomaraswamy identified similarity of the crouching dwarf to 'yaksha-vāhana and to 'kupiro yakho' of Bharhut. Shri Sudhakar Chattopadhyaya calls its Rudra Linga and dated to first century B.C. Shri H. Sarkar took the *liṅga* as a freak creation. Ms. Gritli V. Mitter Wallner dated the figure between 50 B.C. to 50. A.D. Ms. Dorith Meth Srinivasan and N.P. Joshi fixed the date of *liṅga* to third-second century B.C.

Thus, the *liṅga* certainly belongs to 2nd to 3rd century B.C. or to early Sātavāhanas, because, the physiogomy of the figure on the *liṅga* ịs closer to Bharhut, Kārle and Nānāghat figures. Further the practice of worshipping the image in open sky confirms the earliest feature and mode of workship in India.

The image on the *liṅga* may represent Śiva who appeared as Kirāta (hunter) to Arjuna before bestowing Pāśupata weapon. Thus, it may represent Kirāt form of Śiva which was highly praised in the Śatarudrīya.

I feel strongly that the figure on *liṅga* represents Kannappa a tribal who offered his eyes to Śiva with devotion and was recognized as one of the Saiva Nayanar of South India. Thus the Śivalinga represents "Kannappanu grahamūrthi" .

Kannappa, a great hunter used to worship Śiva by offering flesh and wine. One day lord Śiva wanted to test the devotion of Kannappa and shedded tears and blood from his eyes. Kannappa who approached Śiva, saw the blood and made attempts to treat the eye with herbs. Being failed, he offered his own eyes to Śiva and stopped blood comming out from *liṅga.* Śiva being highly pleased with the sacrifice made by Kannappa, bestowed all boons. Thus, finally Kannappa merged in Śiva on account of his absolute devotion. Kannappa was praised by great Śaiva Nāyanārs like Nakkirar besides Sambandār, Appār, Manikkavāsagar, Sundaramūrtī and great Adisankara in Śivāṇandalahari. The story of Kannappa was described in Skānda, Śiva and *Liṅga purāṇas* in glorious terms. Thus, the anthromorphic form depicted on Guḍimallam Śivalinga is that of Kannappa, who approached Śiva with great enthusiasm, whom lord Śiva embraced and merged with himself.

References

1. *Gazetteers of Chitoor Distt.*
2. *Early Saiva Art & Iconography* by Dr. I.K. Sharma
3. *Elements of Iconography* by Gopinatha Rao, vol. I

5

DIETETICS IN ANCIENT ĀNDHRA

"Nagarī nagrsyēva raṭhāsyava rathī yaṭhā
Svaśarīrasya mēdhavī kṛithyēshvavahite bhavet"

Dietetics is a subject intimately connected with the welfare of the king in Ancient India. Sômadēva in his Yaśastilaka describes that king Yaśôgarh, the hero of the kāvya, listens to an exposition on sound dietetics by his royal physician Sajjana as a part of his daily activities. Thus, this text like other literature does not give detailed description of various items of food and their preparation but devotes more to the medical value and suitability to one according to his/ her own nature.

The antiquity of present Karimnagar dates back to the pre-historic times. Sātavāhanas, the earliest historically known dynasty that ruled over Deccan had several important settlements in this district.[1]

This area called Sapadalaksha or Kôśavala or Sabbinādu in ancient period, was ruled over by the Chālukyans of Vēmulawāda, as subordinates of Rāshtrakūṭas. King Vinayāditya Yuddhamallā (750-775 A.D.), the founder of the dynasty accompanied Rāshtrakūṭa Dantidurga in his expedition against the Mālava, Kaliṅga, Gaṅga and Pallava rulers. Another king Arikesari-I (775-800 A.D.) was a learned prince; proficient in grammer, logic, medicine and gajatantra. Narasimha I (800-825 A.D.), Yuddhamalla-II (825-850 A.D.) and Baddega I (50-895 A.D.) were other important kings of this line. King Narasiṁha-II (916-930 A.D.) was a great military leader of the age. His son by a Rāshtrakūṭa princess, named Arikesari-II (930-955 A.D.) also was married to two Rāshtrakūṭa princesses. Arikesari-II was succeeded by Vagarāja and Baddega. During this time Sômadēva Suri, the Jain philosopher and political thinker, probably commenced to write Yaśastilaka, a chaṁpu kāvya at Gaṅgādhara, in present Kurkyala taluk of Karimnagar district and completed the work in 959 A.D. when Arikēśari-III, the last known ruler of this dynasty accompanied Rāshtrakūta Krishna III in his southern expedition[1].

Sômadēva while upholding the Jaina philosophy and religion in his Yasastilaka, incidentally refers to different types of food eaten by various classes of people.

Food Habits of various classes —The meal of the king consisted of white rice, golden yellow broth, fragrant butter, well dressed curries, well cooked dishes, savory, hard curds, sweet milk, milk-rice pudding and water perfumed with camphor[2]. The royal kitchen, used to employ many cooks, a steward and a chief cook and maintain animals and birds like goat, fish, cock, peacock etc. for royal food; the fish was preserved for several days and the slices meat and fish were fried in royal kitchen under special care[3].

The household cooking, water drawing and other menial labour was done by servants in rich houses[4]. The most popular dish sweetmeat ball was prepared with rice flour in sugar syrup[5]. This item was generally given by the mothers to their children, to console them[6]. Papad, made of black gram and ripen mangoes were also liked[7]. The ripen corn, fresh sugarcane juice flavoured with slices of raw ginger were enjoyed in the winter[8], while coconut water was relished in summer[9].

Cooked rice was the main item of every day food, oil was the cooking medium and salt was used as basic material for taste. Probably food was taken on plantain leaves[10].

Generally, rice gruel was taken by the poor[11]; Satku (fried flour with sugar and water), kaṅda (tube), mula (roots) and gruel made from apamārga plant were also used, though the last item was very difficult to digest[12].

A miser, though he could afford to take good meal, used to take the food consisting of rice boiled with full of husk and gravel, rotten beans, few drops of rancid atasi (flax) oil, silces of half cooked gurd, badly cooked vegetable, raw fruits, overburnt brinjals; sour gravel mixed with plenty of mustards, beverage of some alkaline fluid which tasted too salty and boiled black rice (syamli) mixed with butter-milk. Rice mixed with whey was the best item that was offered to a diety in the miser's house[13].

As a Jaina writer, Sômadēva states that a Jaina house holder and monk should take all liquids after straining through cloth. Items like rice-gruel, pickels, syrups, unhusked paddy, flowers, fruits, roots and leaves, oil or water kept in leather bags and flesh should not be used as food since there is possibility of life in these items. The bulbs herbs, pulses, beans and vegetables, be taken only after splitting into two pieces, to check the existence of any living therein. It is stated that a Jaina monk should abstain from taking wine, honey, and fruits of Uḍuṁbara, Aśvattha, Palāsa and Nayagrôdha, as these varieties contain germs[14].

Flourishing dairyfarm, herds of cows, sheep etc., availability of plenty of curds, milk and clarified butter was also mentioned by Sômadēva[15].

A long list of fruits like Arkaphala, Kapiṅgala, Agasthi, Ringiniphala, Chūtasri, Āmrachutaka, Chirabati, Pichumandāra, Bṛihati, Raṅdu, Parāṅdu (Onion), Araṅdu, Mandika, Uḍumbara, Rajika and etc. was given in Yaśastilaka in one context[16].

Though Jainism was very popular in the area during the period under study, the sale of meat and wine was also prevalent. Fisherman and hunters were frequently mentioned in ,the story[17]. It is described that meat juice was prepared and that parched paddy, grain, sour juice of tamarind were used to enhance the taste of wine[18].

Whether it is a common house holder or a king, the offering of food and hospitality to a guest was considered as highly meritorious in those days.

Need for Exercise and Sleep— Sômadēva states that a man who neither exercises nor sleeps cannot digest what he eats, just like food that cannot be cooked well in a vessel that is neither covered nor stirred. The king therefore is advised to go for exercise and wrestling till tired; then to apply and massage oil on body and take bath in swimming pool of his own palace. The king should have pleasant sleep so that his senses (*indriyas*) work properly, his stomach becomes light and the digestive system functions well[19].

Need for Oil Bath—Sômadēva further states that massaging of oil to body removes tiredsomeness, vātavikār, mētha and kapḥ diseases; prevents weakness of the body, makes it strong, and gives luster to the skin. Thus the oil bath gives longivity and improves blood circulation. Both cold and hot water can be used for a bath as per the season. When the body is tired and full of sweat due to hard work, a good bath relieves one from tiredsomeness, induces good sleep and stimulates appetite[20].

Food Etiquette—The king after taking bath, should worship the diety of his choice, offer hospitality to the guests and be in a happy and relaxed disposition. He should dress, decorate himself and get ready to take food in the company of his family members and elose people[21]. Sômadēva states that one should take food when one is really hungry and has appetite as, overindulgence in food awakes the sleeping snakes of diseases in his body[22]. Some contemporary theories regarding proper time for taking food given by experts like Chārāyana, Timi, Mishatismana and Charaka, were referred to by Sômadēva[23]. It is stated finally "The one who knows well the vaidyavidya says that one should not take food during night time while the lotus navel is closed but one should take food during day time when the sun is bright and lotus navel is open[24]."

"Hṛinnābhipadma samkôcha svandarôchana pāyataḥ/
Ātônktaṁ na bhôktavyaṁ vaidya vidyavidām varouḥ //

Thus, observance of nakta or skipping the night meal is suggested as the best method.

Sômadēva states that worship, eating and sleeping should not be performed in open air, in the darkness, at the time of sun-set or sun rise or in a totally covered house. Further, it is stated that while eating, sleeping and attending natural calls the mind should be free and clean. The one who is worried while eating and sleeping will get all types of diseases[25].

The king is advised to offer the food first to those who are along with him so that the evil eyes of others will not affect him. During the course of eating by the king the presence of people who eat leftovers, the opponents, cruel, sick, hungry persons and men of bad character should be avoided[26].

Course of Serving—Eating of food should be begun with tasty and delicious items. It should be followed by soft and heavy items. Then salty and acidic items and finally sour liquid items should be taken. Once the meal is completed no item should be eaten immediately[27].

"Ādu svādu sigdhaṁ guru, madhyē lavadāmlā
onupasēvyām
Ṛkṣmdravaṁ cha pasvanṇ cha bhuktva
bhakṣyokticham"

Vegetables like niṣpāvaka, kôhola, karkata, vārtinka

baṁbhrista kāravālum, chilli and leafy vegetables like rājadolika, Jīvaṅti, bhattanta, svarbhattāta, tāṅduluya, alapamārisham were made into slices, mixed with juice of ginger and served. Because, in a meal all vegetables should be of one fourth of the total quantity food[28].

"Bhôjyasya sarvaśākaṁ samācharet"

The food eaten by the king should be beneficial, good for health, balanced, well cooked, good to look at, good to smell, tasty and tested before serving the king. The food should be eaten neither very slowly nor very fast.

"Hitaṁ, parimitaṁ pakvaṁ, nētranāsāpriyaṁ
Parikṣhitam cha bhujant na dhṛitaṁ, nāvilaṁbitaṁ"

Over-eating, under-eating and eating of food which does not suit one's body should be avoided. The food, that gives strength, life and vitality (balajīvītô pēśālam) only should be taken.

The meal of the king should end with tāmbūla chewing in the company of the beloveds in a happy and relaxed mood enjoying music, pleasant talk or sounds of birds[29].

Sômadēva mentions various items of forbidden food (viparīta bhôjana) like, the reheated food or food prepared longback; all types of sprouted grains (germinating paddy); ghee kept in brass vessel for 10 days; curd with banana; milk with salt; kaṅjika mixed with the juice of kalina fruit; pippali, jaggari, honey and mirch mixed with kākāmarchi; radish with soup of black grams; fried barley powder (satku) which becomes thick like curd; green vegetable and pāpad (mirjala vyanjana) with curd; eating of seasaumum preparations at night, and items kept over night except those prepared in ghee and milk; food containing hair or worms; food which has changed its colour (decoloured); not cooked well, disturbed, emnating bad odour, dried, tasteless, overcooked and that which is not suitable to the body. Further, eating of food immediately after eating and eating of mixture of hygienical and unhygienical food also should be avoided[30]. Thus unclean food should be avoided by the king.

After giving the list of forbidden items of food, Sômadēva gives the tests for the food which should be served to the king. Sômadēva states that crow, cuckoo and cocks, cry and agitate at the sight of poisonous food, while mongoose and peacock jump joyfully. After taking poisonous food, the kraunch bird sleeps, the parrot vomits; the monkey evacuates bowls; the swan or goose limps. The flies do not settle on the poisonous food. Just like salt cracks with the touch of fire, the poisonous food crackles the (king's) human body[31].

"Yadhā lavaṇsdṁparkasputaṁ sputaie pāvakaḥ /
Viṣadashyanāsaṁparakathadha vasumatīpati //

Therefore, after the food is tested and found free from poison, should it be served to the king.

Next, Sômadēva describes the beneficial qualities of ghee, curds, milk and water as well as the bad effect of taking the same in excess or in a wrong method. Fresh cow milk is supposed to be best food as it gives longevity.

"Kṣhīraṁ sākṣajjīvanaṁ"

Drinking of milk in the morning, evening and afternoon is good for health but the milk which is kept for more than 10-20 ghatikas is not good.[32] Eating of curd which is good to look at; smells well; and is tasty is good for health, as it removes dôṣas from body

"Rūpamôdarasādhyam yavatatyadhi prasyaṁ"

Curd mixed with ghee, sugar, āmala, green gram, bitter items is worthy to eat but not in Vasant, Śarad and Grīśma seasons.[33] The butter milk is called "Samaguṇa as it removes all dôṣas.

"Kathayantu samaguṇaṁ
cha na kasya dôṣasya"

The curd is churned well for butter. All eatables prepared in clarified butter on fire are suitable for eating as the ghee gives longevity, stops disease and aging of human beings; so the medical treatises call ghee "rasāynaṁ".

Vedabhirnagditam "sākṣhadihayunirnaṁ"
'yadhoudyesh' 'rasāyanaṁ' pathitam sadhye 'jaranāśanānt'

The learned state that ghee inreases buddhi. Sômadēva states that the ghee which is yellow, like the juice of Kētaki flower, causes happiness and welfare (kalayāṇ)[34].

Water—Sômadēva in Yasastilaka gives guidance on the proper use of water too. Water which is transparent, tasteless and odourless; and swept by wind and light is good for health. The water exposed too much to the rays of the sun and the moon should not be used for more than a day and night; otherwise, water should be boiled before drinking. Water boiled during daytime should not be taken at night and water boiled at night should not be taken during daytime. The water should be sipped during the meal in moderate quantity but drinking in large quantity at a time is not good, for health. Therefore, water is called both amṛita and viṣa, and should be used properly for good results[35].

Water to be taken in different seasons and its sources is also mentioned by Sômadēva[36].

Besides giving the merits of milk and other items, Sômadēva mentions the bad effects of taking some items in excess or in wrong method. It is stated that drinking of too much sweet milk prevents hunger and causes indigestion (agṇimādhya); taking of milk with salt or (lavaṇa) too much salt in food damages the eye sight; eating of too sour and pungent dishes brings quick old age, causes weakens and deteriorates the capacity of assimilation. It is stated that drinking of water soon after coming from scorching heat weakens eye sight; eating of food and drinking of water when one is too tired results in vomiting and fever; drinking of water before taking meal destroys the hunger and shrinks the digestive system; drinking of too much water after meal causes kapha; drinking of water without passing the stool causes disease like gulmi and drinking of water without passing the urine results in the disease bhagaṅdra[37].

Since indigestion is a common health hazard, Sômadēva gives remedies for indigestion too. It is stated that cold water should be taken to be relieved from indigestion caused due to eating of sticky food of yava or like grains, but boiled water should be taken if the indigestion is due to *piṣṭānna* (flour food); boiled rice water (*kaṅjika*) should be taken when indigestion is due to food taken viditakala (delayed food) and butter milk should be taken for the heaviness caused due to taking of improper ghee items[38].

Rasa, Agni and Dôṣas—In the beginning of the discussion on dietetics itself, Sômadēva states that the royal physician Sajjana, who bore a title "Vaidyavidyaviśārada", could produce 63 flavours by means of various combinations of the basic six flavours.

The six basix tastes are madhura, (sweet), āmla (sour), kaṭu (pungent), tikta (bitter), kaṣhāya (astringent) and lavaṇa (salt). The 63 combinations of these six flavours are grouped into different classes depending upon the number of rasas used in each combination[39].

"Rasānām suddha saṁsarga bēdhēna/
trisaṣti vyaṅjnôpadēsabhajaḥ Sajianabhi shajaḥ" //

Sômadēva while referring to food states that men are classified as per the nature of their hunger, which is of four types : (1) mandajatharāgni (2) tīkṣaṇa jaṭharāgni (3) viṣhamajaharāgni (4) samajaṭharāgni and which require light, heavy, soft and normal food successively[40].

"Maṅdatīkṣaṇanôviṣamaḥ saṁsvā vahnisvatu
chaturvidḥ puṁsam/
Laghu maṅda guru tīkṣaṇôsnigdhaṁ
viṣame samaṁ chadyat.//

The three basic dôṣas of human body i.e. vāta, pitta, vāyu and different movements as anchaya, prakôpa, prasama of dôṣas in different seasons were[41] explained by Sômadēva as follows :

"Śaśir surabhi gharmsyā tāpāmbḥ śarastu"
kṣhitipa jalaśardvhēmaṅtakālēṣuchoutē /
kapḥpāvanhutāsaḥ saṅchayaṁ cha prakôpam
prasmih. bajante jarmabajamkramenaḥ//

It is stated that one should take all rasas (food) in suitable quantity, suitable to each season, depending upon the state of dôṣas of his own body and health in order to balance the[42] effects of the dôṣas and to keep good health.

Food in different seasons—The medicinal values of food (change of rasas) with reference to the nature of human body and the changing environment are described by Sômadēva. It is stated that in autumn, one should take sweet, bitter and astringent things and diet should consist of ghee, soup of green gram, śalī rice, powdered wheat, preparations of milk, patolas, grapes, amalaki fruits, sugar, and sweet bulbs and leaves. In the spring season pungent, bitter and astringent things should be taken and the food should consist chiefly of barley, wheat and little ghee. Heavy, cold and sweet dishes are to be avoided. In summer mild preparations like śāli rice, soup of gram containing ghee, lotus stalks, fresh shoots and bulbs, fried barley flour, pānakaṁs (cold drinks), curds mixed with sugar and spices, coconut-milk and water or milk with plenty of sugar are to be taken. In rainy season sweet, salty and sour things, warm, dry, light food, preparations of old śāli rice, wheat and barley should be taken. In winter fresh food, preparations of milk, black gram, sugarcane, curds and things prepared with ghee and oil with sweet, salt and sour taste are beneficial.

The above references made by Sômadēva to 4 types of jaṭharāgni, 3 types of dôṣas and their 4 states in different seasons, 63 types of rasas and to the seasonal and forbidden food in Yasastilaka have medical bearing. Therefore, a backdrop on ancient medical sciences on these aspects is given below.

According to the āyurvedic system of medicine, the human body consists of "Pañchamahābhūtas" (five elements): Pṛithvi (earth) in the form of muscles, fat, tissues; Āp (water) in the form of lymph and other fluids; Tējas (fire) in the form of homaeglobin of blood and enzyme; vāyu (wind) in the form of bones; Ākāśa (ether) in the form of body pores. These five elements are to be substituted in the body by means of food and drinks. Tḥe inbalance results in disease.

The five elements exist in the human body in the form of dôṣas, dhātu and mala also. The 3 dôṣas (natural forces) namely vāyu (wind) pitta (bile) and kapha (phelgm), when exist in normal state, the health will be normal but when exist in three disturbed leavels or states i.e aggravate or excited, vitate and alleviate, cause disease. The three dôṣas govern the physical, psychological and chemical activities of the body. Vāyu dominated by vāyu and ākāśa mahābhūtas is responsible for all the movements, sensation and physical activities. Pitta dominated by tējas is responsible for physio-chemical activities, metabolism and produces heat and energy. Kapha dominated by pṛithvi and Āp maintains composition of body and provide fluid matrix. Therefore, by means of food, exercise and recreation, these elements are to be balanced by every human being.

The concept of rasas (taste) has a vital importance in ancient medicine. It is believed that the tastes of sweet and sour are dominated by prithvi and ap; sour (acid) by āp and tējas; saline by prithvi and tējas; acrid or pungent by vāyu and tējas; bitter by vāyu and ākāśa; astrigent by vāyu and pṛithvi. Further, it is stated that the sweet, sour and the saline check the vāyu dôṣas; the astrigent, sweet and the bitter check pitta dôṣas; stringent (or acrid), pungent and the bitter check kapha dôṣas.

That is why, particular type of food dominated[43] by a particular rasa has been prescribed to be eaten in each season, so as to balance the body with changing environment and dôṣas. According to ancient writers, in winter due to exposure of body to the cold air, kapha accumulates; the food should be heavy, sweet, and oily like cakes, milk pudding etc. In spring kapha accumulated in winter will be excited and vitiated by the exposure to sun rays, so easily digestible food of pungent, bitter, astringent and saline tastes are to be taken. In summer, sweet, cool, oily food, śāli rice, ghee, milk and lot of drinks and light exercises like excursion to garden and river banks are good for health. Vāyu dôṣas accumulate in summer. In rainy season the vāyu accumulated during summer becomes excited and the digestive fire becomes very weak. Therefore, light, easily digestive food like old barley, rice and wheat, oily food and items of sour and saline taste should be taken. Physical exercise and honey will be useful. In autumn, the pitta accumulated in rainy season becomes excited due to contact with the sun. Therefore, easily digestable food of sweet and bitter taste are beneficial[44]. Thus the collision of the body with the time and diet should be avoided.

Even though the environment, the human body and the diet all are constituted of pañchmahābhūtas only, they exist in human body in a particular ratio and in a state of equillibrium. The equillibrium should be maintained by every individual by doing proper activities suitable to each season and by taking proper food meant for each season of course depending upon one's own nature. Otherwise the equillibrium of the paṅchmahābhūtas within and around the body will be disturbed and result in unhealthyness and diseases. The time, body, mind and objects around should be always in a harmonious state.

This is the reason why Sômadēva like other ancient scholars and philosophers laid importance on the sound dietetics and exercise for the welfare of the king (the earthy god) since he has to look after the welfare of the whole country, the summum bonum of his life.

Seasons and Dôṣas

Seasons	Kaph	Vāyu	Pitta
1. Śisir	Saṅchaya	Prakôpa	Prasama
2. Vasant	Prakôpa	Prasama	Saṅchaya
3. Grīshma	Prasama	Saṅchaya	Prakôpa
4. Varṣhā	Sanchaya	Prakôpa	Prasama
5. Śarad	Prakôpa	Prasama	Saṅchaya
6. Hēmant	Prasama	Saṅchaya	Prakôpa

The list of 63 combination of six Rasas— Madhurāmla; Kaṭutikta; Kaṭukaṣāya; Tiktakaṭu; Kaṣaya; Katukaṣāya; Madhurāmla; Madhura lavaṇa; Madhura tikta; Madhura kaṭu; Madhura kaṣāya; Āmla lavaṇa; Āmla kaṭu; Āmla tikta; Āmla kaṣāya; Lavaṇa tikta; Lavaṇa kaṭu; Lavaṇa kaṣāya; Tikṭa kaṭu; Tikta Kaṣāya; (*Pachadasa*) (Total 20 Rasas)

Madhurāmla lavaṇāni; Madhurāmla tiktāni; Madhurāmla kaṭukāni; Madhurāmla kaṣāyāni; Madhuramla lavaṇa tiktāni; Madhura lavaṇa kaṭukāni; Madhura lavaṇa kaṣāyāni; Madhura tiktāni; Madhura tikta kasāyāni; Madhura kaṭukāṣāni. (Total 10 Rasas)

Āmla lavaṇa tiktakaṣāyāni; Āmla tiktāni; Āmla lavaṇa kaṣāyāni; Āmla tikta kaṭukāni; Āmla tikta kaṣāyāni; Āmla kaṣāyāni; (Total 6 Rasas)

Lavaṇa tikta kaṭukāni; Lavaṇa tikta kaṣāyāni; Lavaṇa kaṭu kaṣāyāni; Lavaṇa tikta lavaṇa kaṣāyāni; (Total 4 Rasas)

Madhura āmla lavaṇa tiktāni; Madhura āmla lavaṇa kaṭukāni; Madhura lavaṇa kaṣāyāni; Madhura lavaṇa tikta kaṣāyāni; Madhura lavaṇa kaṭu kaṣāyāni; Madhura tikta kasāyāni; Madhura āmla tikta kaṭukāni; Madhura āmla tikta kaṣāyāni; Madhura āmla lavaṇa kaṭukāni; Madhura lavaṇa tikta kaṭukāni; (Total 10 Rasas)

Āmla lavaṇa tikta kaṭukāni; Āmla lavaṇa kaṣāyāni; Āmla lavaṇa kaṣāyāni; Āmla lavaṇa tikta kaṭu kaṣāyāni; Lavaṇa tikta kaṭu kaṣāyāni; (Total 5 Rasas)

Āmla lavaṇa tikta kaṭu kaṣāyāni; Madhura tikta lavaṇa kaṣāyāni; Madhura tikta kaṭu kaṣāyāni; Madhura āmla tikta kaṭu kaṣāyāni; Madhura āmla lavaṇa tikta kaṣāyāni; Madhura āmla lavaṇa tikta kaṭukāni; (Total 6 Rasas)

Madhura āmla lavaṇa tikta kaṭu kaṣāyāni; (Total 1 Rasa)

(This article was read in 16th session of Āndhra Pradesh History Congress 1992.)

References

1. Historical introduction: Inscriptions of Āndhra Pradesh (Karimnagar District), Epigraphical series No. 8, Govt. of Āndhra Pradesh, Hyderabad and also see Handiqui, K.K., *Yaśastilaka and Indian Culture*, Sholapur, Year 1949 pps 2-5. The inscriptions of the Chāḷukyans of Vemulawada found in Karimnagar distt. so far published refer to donations made to the feeding houses (sattra) for the sake of asceties, jaina munis, poor, quests and pilgrims of both brahmanical and Jaina sects, but do not provide details of food items or related matters.
2. Handiqui, K.K., *Yasastilaka and Indian Culture* p. 29
3. *Ibid* pps 38, 81, 419 and 425.
4. *Ibid* p. 31.
5. *Ibid* pps 15, 78 and 422
6. *Ibid* p. 80.
7. *Ibid* p. 418.
8. *Ibid* p. 162.
9. *Ibid* p. 158
10. *Ibid* pps 70, 71 and 427.
11. *Ibid* p. 35.

12. *Ibid* p. 69.
13. *Ibid* pps. 29 and 70.
14. *Ibid* pps 262, 263 and 264.
15. *Ibid* pps. 58, 71, 72 and 421.
16. *Ibid* p. 70.
17. *Ibid* pps. 37, 40, 41, 62, 84, 63, 116, 418 and 419.
18. Sômadēva Suri., The Yasastilaka with commentary of Srutadeva Suri edited by Mahamahopadhyaya Pandit Śivadatta and Vasudeva Laxman Sastri Panasikar, pt. I Book III, Year 1916, Vs.nos. 62-418.
19. *Ibid* pp. 332 and 322.
20. *Ibid* V. Nos. 323, 324 and 325.
21. *Ibid* V. No. 327.
22. *Ibid* V. No. 329.
23. *Ibid* V. Nos. 328 and 330.
24. *Ibid* V. No. 331.
25. *Ibid* V. Nos. 332 and 334.
26. *Ibid* V. Nos. 333 and 335.
27. *Ibid* V. No. 346.
28. *Ibid* V. Nos. 356 and 357.
27. *Ibid* V. Nos 337, 345 and 372-74. After meal anger, hardwork, travel, riding, exposure to heat should be avoided.
30. *Ibid* V. Nos. 341, 342, 343, 344, 336 and 357.
31. *Ibid* V. Nos. 338, 339 and 340.
32. *Ibid* V. No. 363.
33. *Ibid* V. Nos. 361, 358 and 361.
34. *Ibid* V. Nos. 359 and 360.
35. *Ibid* V. Nos. 370, 371 and 368.
36. *Ibid* V. No. 369. Water from well in Vasant and Grisma seasons; from chodya (etam) in rainy season; from ponds & lakes in winter, and all types of water in Saral season are good for health.
37. *Ibid* 364, 365, 367, 368 and 326.
38. *Ibid* V. No. 366.
39. *Ibid* V. No. 320 commentary of Srutasagara and p. 52.
40. *Ibid* V. No. 347.
41. *Ibid* V. Nos. 348 and 355.
42. Ibid V. Nos. 349 and 354.
43. Shri Bhagawan Dash and Lalitesh Kashyap, *Materia Medica of Ayurveda* based on Ayurveda Saukhyam of Todarananda (New Delhi Year 1980 introduction)
44. Sengupta, K.N.N., *The Ayurvedic system of Medicine*.

6

SASYAKRĪḌA

The Chāḷukyas of Kalyāṇi ruled over Kuṅtala Dēśa, present State of Karnataka from c 973 A.D. to c 1192 A.D. extending their power to several parts of Āndhra, Dravida, Mahārāshṭra and Madhya Dēśas. King Sômeśvara III (A.D. 1126-A.D. 1138) of this dynasty was a lover of letters than war and politics; so engaged himself in composing a treatise entitled *"Mānasôllāsa"* (the refresher of the mind) during A.D. 1129-A.D. 1130 enjoying the prosperous kingdom inherited from his father. The Mānasôllāsa comprising of 100 chapters, grouped into five books of twenty each, is encyclopaedic in nature; throws a flood of light on the personality of the ruling king, court life as well as on the contemporary culture and technical subjects.[1]

Sômeśvara in his Mānasôllāsa describes a pastime called 'Sasyakrīḍa'. As the name suggests, this is a krīḍa, enjoyed by the king in beautiful green fields full of crop/harvest (paddy), in Hemanta season;[2] when the elephants play and swans move freely in lotus ponds; the cranes and sāraṅga birds flutter; the lotuses dry, the feathers of peacocks drop, the deers are troubled; the moonlight is white and clear like camphor, when kuṅda flowers; the air is fragrant with the smell of gandhaśāli rice; men shiver due to cold winds and go near fire to warm themselves and when lovers enjoy long nights.[3]

Hēmante sasya śālinī krīḍa
Kurvat bhūpāle ramyakṣhētrasamasritaṁ

(V. No. 5.9.345 & 346)

The field of paddy/farms where the king plays the krīḍa are maintained with fresh grass, and tender seedlings which look like parrot feather (on which the king walks) besides a variety of fruit bearing and flowering trees; without any sticky mud and bad odour. The whole environs look green even without the arrival of spring season. Further, the area is protected by faithful servants of the king.[4]

Before the king reaches the sasyakrīḍa kṣētra (farm), the cooks who reached the place early, prepare and keep ready various items of food like dadyôdana (curd rice) mixed with ginger, yēla, mārichi and āmla, wheat gruel, pôlika, saspali; pupala (sweet pūrī), pāyasam made of sugar; honey, vegetables, wine, buttermilk, curds, rahizom, roots, fruits, salt, rajika and eatable made of the meat of sheep and pig.[5]

The king arrives at the place of entertainment in a pleasant mood accompanied by brāhmins, queens, lovers, friends, dancers and bodyguards.[6] He is welcomed by erecting a gateway made of freshly plucked green plants, amidst sweet sounds of the instruments (veeṇa) and melodious songs. The king enters the area through the gateway all alone;

"Avakāsārth mutpādhyā tatra sasyāni kaṅichit
Chaturaśram viśālam cha kuryādramyā pravēśakam"

(V. No. 5.9. 401)

Then, the brāhmins, queens, lovers, dancers, singers and others follow with eagerness, obedience and happiness.[7]

When everybody settled, the king offers tasty food prepared from kalaya, siṁbika, wheat spike, niṣhpāva grains; karkātika fruits and other items to the brāhmins, lovers and servants separately;[8] then takes his food in happy disposed alongwith sons and relatives.[9] At the end, the king throws/offers food on all sides for the deity presiding over the field.[10]

'Tatah kṣhētradhidēvôbhyaḥ kirēdannaṁ samantataḥ"

(V.No. 5.9. 407)

Besides, the tender top parts of the gram plants which are red in colour and sour in taste are plucked and mixed with hīng, plain salt, jeera, pepper powder and blended by adding a little oil and powder of sṛingavera. The same is packed in various beautiful packets made of leaves of simbika or niṣpāva and heated in the fire made of dry stems, leaves and cowdung cakes collected then and there itself.[10a]

"Kilitāni suramyāni sthālyāvaṭparikalpayēt"

(V. No. 5.9. 408)

When the mixture within the leave packets is cooked well, is served to all. Afterwards, the gram (*chaṇaka*) plants which are full of fruits are fried on the flames; and the fried gram fruits cleaned from the ashes is offered to the king who eats the same for taste and excitement along with followers.[11] The gram cooked in salt water is also distributed to all. The corn is fried on fire, the dust is removed with hands by winnoing gently; these tender seeds full of milky juice, which look like parrot feather are also enjoyed by the king in the company of his sons, grandsons and others.[12] Thereafter, madira is offered to the king as anupāna.[13] The other items like butter milk with salt; the dhyôdana; mixture of tender fruits of khalaka, kākaḍi, bṛihati, karpas, vārtika, vēlam, the tender leaves of thīkṣhnaka, mandika, kushuṁbha; red carrote, kaṅḍa, mūla, phala as well as the pieces of ksitaki fruits mixed with the powder of mustered and salt; and fried meat of pig and sheep are savoured by the king, freely.[14]

After the completion of food, the king rests in the form

(green lawns) for some time; adorns himself and leaves for his palace in the company of queens and lovers on the best horse which is decorated with golden ornaments and silk cushion.[15]

The roots of sasyakrīḍ described above may be traced back to the Vēdic agricultural and seasonal rites and sacrifices. In the Vēdic literature, the field and furrow were described as presided over by Kṣētrapati[16] and Sītā respectively; ôṣadhis, Sôma creeper and vegetation were highly praised.[17] Some periodical rites and sacrifices were performed in connection with different stages of agricultural operations (Ṛgveda II 57). At the time of first motion of the plough (ayôjara), lāṅgala yajña or halābhiyanja was performed to satisfy Parjanya, Bhāga and Indra in the field itself. Similarly, Sīta yajña was offered to Sīta, the goddesses of furrow; Sthālīpaka was offered to Kṣētrapati the deity of the field and Khalā yajña was offered while thrashing the floor. So also rites were performed at the time of sowing the seeds (Pravapana), reaping of the crop (Pralavaṇa) and putting the corn in barn (Prayayaṇa).[18]

Before partaking the stored grain, the Agrāyana iṣṭi was performed in each season sacrificing the same to Indra, Agṇi, Annapati, Vaiśvadēvas, Dhanvantari, Earth and Heaven. The Āgrayaṇi iṣṭi performed on full moon day of Mārgaśira in autumn, was called "Navasasyēṣṭi" by Manu.[19]

Besides the rites mentioned above, a householder used to perform the Chāturmāsya iṣṭi at the beginning of spring, mansoon and autumn seasons, Maruts being the principal deity of worship besides, Agṇi, Sôma, Sāvitṛ and Pūsan. The wood of the tree, which blossoms in that particular season was used for making the fire wood and the plant that sprouts at that time has for brahvis in chāturmāsyas. In the course of Sākamēdha the chaturmasya the yāgnas was performed in autumn; offerings were made to Śunāsira (plough or essence); and the iṣṭi ended with festivity.[20] So also, at the time of Prātyaurôhaṇa ceremony performed at each season, adornments appropriate to that season were used and food of the season was offered to the brāhmins.[21]

The above references made to the significance of the seasonal grain and vegetation in gṛihya rites, reveal that at agrarian stage, man being dependent on nature for his existence and security, regarded the vegetation and crop as highly precious and offered sacrifices.

But in course of time the society has undergone several changes. Therefore, the purāṇas propagated different types of worship/rites, stating that the vedic rites prescribed by Manu cannot be performed in Kali age.[22]

Maṅtrayajñapara viprah sītyājña cha karṣhakaḥ
giriyjñastatha gôparijgô samabhīr girirvanē.

Harivamsapurāṇa : 2.16.9

Accordingly the mode of offering of the yajñas, the seasonal rites including those of agriculture developed as social activities and festivals (Mahās). The Viṣṇupurāṇa calls folk festivals (Mahā) as yajña;[23] thus by the end of ancient period, the vedic rites changed their form as festivals but retaining the original essence and spirit.

In Deccan, the agricultural rites/festivity like Sasyesti took the form of Sasyakrīḍ perhaps. Several features like preparation of food in field itself, offering of seasonal food to Keṣtērapati, the brāhmans and others; eating of seasonal food by the king in the company of sons and grandsons in the field, the use of freshly plucked green plants for welcoming the king, making the bowls with green leaves for cooking the gram described in Mānasôllāsa are some of the relics of vedic agricultural rites.[24]

Thus, the boundaries of religious and social activities are very much blurred because the term ritual itself is derived from the Latin word 'ritus' meaning a custom and the religious ceremony which when becomes a routine, forms a feature of social life.

(This article was read in 52nd session of Indian History Congress 1992.)

References

1. Yazdani (ed.), The Early History of the Deccan pts I-VI pps 370-372 and 453.
2. Sômeśvaraś Mānasôllas, Vol. III Gaekwad's Oriental Series Baroda, 1961 V Nos 5.9. 380; 385 and 86.
3. *Ibid* V. Nos. 381-385.
4. *Ibid* V. Nos. 387-395.
5. *Ibid* V. Nos. 395-398.
6. *Ibid* V. Nos. 398-400.
7. *Ibid* V. Nos. 400-402.
8. *Ibid* V. Nos. 403 and 404.
9. *Ibid* V. Nos. 405.
10. *Ibid* V. Nos. 407.

10a. *Ibid* V. Nos. 408-411.

11. *Ibid* V. Nos. 413.
12. *Ibid* V. Nos. 412-413 & V. Nos. 415-16-17.
13. *Ibid* V. Nos. 417-418.
14. *Ibid* V. Nos. 418-421.
15. *Ibid* V. Nos. 422-425.
16. Macdonell's, *Vedic Mythology*-p. 138; and also Vyas's India as known to Ramayana p. 83; Hopkin's *Epic Mythology*, pps 72, 79 and 99. Agarwala, V.S. - *Folk Cults* - pps 114-135.
17. *Ibid* pps 154-86 and Grisworld pps 306-307.
18. *Cultural Heritage of India* Vol. I Ramakrishna Mission, Calcutta; pps 255-56 and Ram Gopal's *India in the Vedic Kalpasūtras*; pps 425-35.
19. Ram Gopal-*India in the Vedic Kalpasūtras*, Delhi, 1959; pps. 425-30; Kane, P.V. *History of Dharma Sāstras*, Pune, Vol. II, Pt. II p. 827.
20. *Ibid* - pps 424-426 and the *Religion and Philosophy of the Vēdas and Upaniṣhad* by Arthur Berriedale Keith: Oxford University, Year 1925 pps 321-323 and 324; the *Cultural Heritage of India* Vol. I Calcutta pps 249-50.
21. Ram Gopal; *India in Vedic Kalpasūtras* p. 414 and Kane, P.V., *History of Dharma Śāstras* Vol. II Pat. II p. 827.
22. Padmapurāna (VI 53.4 to 6); The *Harivaṁsa purāṇa* (2.16.9)
23. The Śatapatha Brāhmaṇa (1.9.11) also states that yajñas has the same significance for Dēvas as Mahā for the people; "Yajñavai Dēvanammahā".
24. *Encylopaedia of Religion and Ethics* and Oxford Dictionary.

7

THE SYMBOLIC MEANING OF VOTIVE TANKS

The votive tanks which have been brought to light during the course of excavations in different parts of India throw a challenge to the excavators in regard to the contextual interpretation.

The so called votive tanks or terracotta miniature tank like boats have been noticed in the length and breadth of Indian sub-continent; from Taxila in north to Arikamedu in south; from Surkotada in west to Rajgir in east during a long span of period extending from 3rd or 2nd century B.C. to the 4th century A.D.

The votive tanks found so far, are rectangular, squarish, oval or circular in shape with a wall or rim applied with lamps as found at Taxila, Ahar, Ahichchhatra, Ujjain, Bairat, Sambhar, Navadatoli, Nala Sopara, Paunar, Bhokardan, Ter, Rangamahal and Brahmapuri. The tanks are with a flight of steps on one side of the walled enclosure as found at Taxila, Rajghat, Navadatoli, Nevasa, Bhokardan, Paunar, Ter, Kaundinyapura and Brahmapuri. Mostly the tanks have birds with spread-out wings, perching on the rim as noticed at Taxila, Ahichchhatra, Sambhar, Bhokardan, Kaundinyapura and Brahmapuri; or with aquatic animals and snakes on the floor as observed at Taxila, Bhita, Sambhar,

Bhokardan, Paunar, Ter, Rairh, Ujjain and at Brahmapuri. At times, drummers or musicians having foreign features are noticed at Ahichchhatra, Hastinapur and Chirand; even a female figure with archaic features is found at Taxila, Ujjain, Ahichchhatra, Ter and Brahmapuri. A separate enclosure or shrine is attached to one side of the tank at Taxila, Bhita, Rairh and Ter; even a roof of a house-like arrangement at Taxila, Sonkh, Sambhar, Ter and Bhita is noticed.

Thus, the lamps, steps, birds and aquatic creatures are some of the common features seen in tanks discovered from almost all sites. The presence of drummers is seen in a rectangular tank from Taxila (Sirkap). In the early examples from Bihr Mound where the votive tank is circular in shape, a series of lamps are decorated on the rim. The circular type continues at Sirkap, Ahar, Sambhar, Ujjain, Paunar, etc. but the rectangular or squarish is prevalent type. The roof-house type is not very common. One among the specimens from Bhita, shows a unique type with attached shrine and seven figurines.

Generally, the votive tanks are associated with proto or early historical period, i.e. first millennium B.C. and which is associated with the tribes mentioned in vedic literature (3000 B.C. - 1500 B.C.) by some scholars; these in later period are called mahājanapadas and are mentioned in Buddhist literature. The early historical period is indicated by the usage of coinage, presence of highways, promotion of trade, use of script and fortified cities. Some of the important sites identified with the capitals of mahājana-pādas are Champā (Aṅga), Vaiśalī (Licchavis), Rājgir (Magadha), Rājghāt (Kāśī), Kauśambī (Vatsa), Śrāvastī (Kôśala), Ahichchhatra (Pāñchāla), Hastināpura (Puru), Mathura (Sūraśena) and Ujjain (Avanti). All these sites except Champā, Vaiśālī and Śrāvastī have yielded early historical relics including the votive tanks. Two of the mahājanapādas Gandhāra and Taxila are located in present Pakistan.

The mahājanapādas are the centres of second urbanisation or the centres of the revival of Harappan culture according to some scholors.

Though the votive tanks are associated with the early historic towns which are identified with fortifications located on river banks, trade and NBPW, all sites, however, did not yield the votive tanks.

For example, the sites of NBPW like Kumarahar, Chechar, Vaiśalī in Bihar; Chandraketugarh, Tāmralipti in Bengal and Champa did not yield votive tanks so far.

Similarly, Bharuch, Somnath, Amreli and Nagara the trade centre of west coast in Gujarat did not reveal any votive tanks.

However, it has been noticed that the votive tanks are found at the sites associated with chalcolithic and megalithic remains. For example Maheswar, Navasa, the chalcolithic sites in Maharashtra; Bhrahmagiri in Karnataka and Arikamedu in Tamil Nadu, the two megalithic sites in south yielded votive tanks.

The chalcolithic period is followed by PGW and NBPW at Ujjain and Besanagar in central India. These places also have yielded the votive tanks. While at Eran from central India, the NBP alongwith votive tanks have been noticed, Tripuri, a nearby place did not show the remains of the votive tanks.

More or less all the sites in central India (Vidarbha) region like Maheswar Eran; Adam, Pauni, Kolhapur, and Ter in Maharashtra yielded both votive tanks and Roman material like coins and Megarian Ware. The whole region was dominated by NBPW.

No site in Bengal or in Orissa has yielded these votive tanks.

Coming to Āndhra region, Palaeolithic, Neolithic, Chalcolithic and Megalithic cultural sequences as well as the early historic to medeival cultural periods are found in continuation at Eleswaram (2000 B.C.). But a little variations in the cultural sequence is found at Nagarjunakonda. These two sites situated on the either bank of river Krishna yielded votive tanks at Sātavāhana levels.

In Karnataka out of many iron yielding megalithic burials, votive tanks are found at Chandravali and Brahamgiri only. Though Sātavāhana sites at Banavasi, Sannati, Vadagaon Madhavpur revealed Roman trade, no votive tank is found so far. Similarly, though flourishing trade was recorded between Tamil Nadu, cost and countries of east and west, a few votive tanks' pieces are found at Arikamedu and Kanchipuram only.

Now, what is this votive tank? What is its significance? Various scholars expressed their opinions on the meaning and purpose of the votive tanks.

Sir John Marshall suggested that the votive tanks may be associated with the Yamapukar rites performed by unmarried girl of Bengal; but unfortunately not even single votive tank is found in the eastern part of the country. Scholars like Sri Aggarwal and Dr. Sankalia considered that the votive tanks originated from Partiharas, as a feature brought from Seleucia and that the human figures represent mother goddess. But the votive tanks are not found in any specific place of worship or in any associated object of worship in any of the sites excavated so far. Shri Puri suggested that the tanks may indicate the consecreation of or the rites associated with the dedication of the tank; but none of the sites mentioned above yielded votive tanks in the tanks excavated so far indicating the connection between the votive tanks and the rites. Votive tanks are not found in any of the reservoirs excavated so far at the sites of mahājanapādas. Shri Puri gave another suggestion that the votive tanks are connected with trade or conveyance.

Sir Marshall also suggested another view that the votive

tanks may be associated with Buddhist or Jaina worship, since these objects are found neạr stupas at Taxila, Pauni, Devanimori, Bhokardan and Eleswaram. It is a well known fact that the Buddhist were mostly engaged in trade as depicted in early art and literature.

The theory that the so called votive tanks are connected with trade and conveyance may be more reasonable and convincing. The votive tanks may represent trade and safe travel on waters or even the export of animals from India to West Asia, Far-east and Near-east countries. The following points support this view.

One terracotta amulet from Mohanjadaro (2500 B.C.) represents figure of a boat having two birds inside (Mackey 1938 PP340-1, Pl. LXX111-30). The vedas refers to the trade on sea and narrates how the merchant Bhuju was saved from shipwreck by birds and helped to reach the shore. The Baudhāyana sūtras R.V.1.116.3-5 B.S.S.-18.40. give the mantras to be recited while loading the boat. The Baveru Jātaka tells that the merchants used to carry birds alongwith them to know the directions; and about the voyage of Indian merchants to Babylonia where Indian crows and peacocks were very much admired. Thus the votive tanks which represent a shrine and a cabin may represent the tower wherefrom the sailor watches the route.

In the light of the above points we can safely say that the votive tanks represent the symbol of trade; the birds on votive tanks indicate the "Diśā-kākas" and the acquatic animals may symbolise the totam for the safe journey on the water, or the export of animals to foreign countries, a practice followed from times of Harappans and in the times of Vēdas and Jātakas. By the time of the early historic period when the trade was carried on large scale and more technical knowledge developed, the votive tank with birds and animals became the symbolic representation of the trade.

The story found in Bible wherein Gilgamesh was helped

by the birds to know the direction at the time of flood also shows the universal practice of the Diśā-kākas.

India and trade with other countries

India has cultural and trade relations with outside world since times immemorial. Generally, it is believed that Mohenjodaro and Harappan civilizations had connections with other countries. The Aryans too had contacts with other countries as referred in the Boghazkui inscription (1360 BC). Vēdas the earliest scripture of India and the Jewish and Iranian literature are supposed to be parallel developments and interlinked due to similarities in these texts. As a matter of human behaviour and development of dynamic nature, the earliest man travelled not only by land but also followed the course of river and wanted to cross even the sea. As a result navigation developed. (*Cultural Heritage of India* Vol I PP 110-120)

The Mesopotomia and Indus seals show that seaborn trade from Tigris to western coast of India was known (Mackay p. 140 Keith p.614). Thus, inhabitants of Harappan site had trade links with Mesopotamia, Sumer, Persia, Iraq, Egypt, Greece and Central Asia. The sea routes were taken from the mouth of Sindhu to Persian Gulf then to Eupheates, Seleucia, Arabia-Suez. The cruciform inscriptions of the 3rd millennium B.C. mentioned the items imported to Mesopotamia. Also the cylindrical seal of Harappa found at Meson and Saragon (Assyria) (2300-2000 B.C.) reflect the trade links between India and other countries (*Cultural Heritage of India* Vol. I pp .147-159).

Coming to below the Vindhyas, the chalcolithic culture of central India had contact with *Ur* (4500 B.C.), as revealed from pottery, terracotta and beads. The megalithic cultures of the Karnataka and Āndhra were supposed to have common features with *Urine* culture (2000 B.C. - 1000 B.C.). (*Ibid*-p. 126-127)

Indian Lapislazuli was supplied for Sumerian jewellery,

also amazonite from central India was exported to Mesopotamia. The Indus seals, carnelian beads and pottery of Indian type are found at Sumerian and Elamite site, and Indian animals like monkey, elephant, rhinocerous, gharial were found in the tombs of Ur and Tell Asmar. Similarly cotton was exported from India to Sumer.

Not only similiarities in archaeological material, but the documents of Babylonia and Asia minor reveal the contacts with India. Kassite documents from Babylonia (Iraq) (C.1760 B.C.) refers to the introduction of horse drawn chariots to Babylonia, which was very familiar to Vedic period. Tel-el-Amarna tablet (1460 B.C.) of Mittani king and the Boghazkui inscription (Turkey) dated 14th century B.C. of Hittite king refers to Indian name and to horse breeding. This is a cruciform inscription and the earliest Indo European record. The Mittanis are supposed to be remnants of Indo-Aryan folk so-called Hurrians (Cultural heritage p.148). Further the Hurrian language has similarities to Sanskrit; it flourished near Greece and Syria in 2nd millennium B.C.

King Solomon in 10th century B.C. stated as had imported gold, sandalwood, precious stones, ivory, peacocks and apes from India. Trade of teakwood, sandalwood took place between Broah and Euphrates even upto 2nd century AD. The Jewish annals refer Indian gods and cultural links between Iran and India. The pre-historic period pottery motifs and types of vessels had common or close connections between Iranian or Pahalvi cultures. In the times of Achaemanian ruler of Iran and that of Darius, their power extended up to Sindh in 6th cent. B.C. and these kings influenced India through Azarian and Kharoṣti words or record. Sophocles (495-405 B.C.) mentions that rice, peacocks and sandalwood were supplied to Greeks by the Indians. So also Hemdotus (484 B.C.) gives a voyage from Sindh to Persian Gulf and trade of crafts, cotton, bamboos and gold (*Cultural Heritage of India* p.126 & 149).

Aromatics, spices and elephants were specifically exported to the *Sassrians* from India. The products like timber of all kinds from India were paid as a tribute to Tigbih Pileser-III (745-727 B.C.) In the parts of the palace of Marcherib Assarian king Ninevah (704-681 B.C.) tree of cotton from India was planted. Similarly, in the temple of moon at Mughar at *Urs*, and in the palace of Nebuchadnezzar; Indian Teak was discovered (606-581 B.C.). The Arabian merchants took Indian goods to Syria and Egypt (*Cultural Heritage of India*, p.149-158).

According to the tablet of Nippur, now kept in the Pannynsylvani University of U.S.A.; a colony of South Indians was developed in the Babylonia and birds, ivory were exported to Babylonia. So also the evidence of Indian species are found in Elam, Urs, Kish even in pre-Sargoric period (2350 B.C.). Indian muslin, monkey, sandalwood, precious stones, elephants and teak were exported to Egypt in 2nd millennium B.C. India had trade with Africa, Madagascar from Mangalore, Pillak and Syria worked as middle man and prospered. The Baveru Jataka narrates that Indian merchants went on long voyages to Baveru, Babylonia and Indian crow and peacock were very much admired there.

Coming to Deccan, Maski had trade of gold with mediterranian countries. Sir John Marshall was of opinion that the gold ornaments discovered at Mohenjodaro were made of gold mined in the Deccan, as revealed by the chemical analysis of the metal used. In the beginning, the Egyptians and the Arabs acted as middlemen and conveyed these goods to Roman merchants and distributors. According to the Periplus Indian commodities were sold in Roman markets at hundred times of their original price. Immense quantities of spices flowed into the Deccan from Europe in exchange for Indian merchandise. After the conquest of Egypt in 30 B.C. by Octovius (Augustus), the Romans established direct commerce with the western part of India. In this connection, many Indian colonies were developed in different parts of the world. Alongwith the western borderland of the Deccan plateau, there were a number of market towns like Paithan, Tagara, Nanaghat, Karle, Junnar, Nasik, Vaijayanti, Broach (Barygaza) Sopara and Kalyana. On the eastern side, Amaravati, Kudura Kontakossyla (Ghantasala) Gudur and Masolia are the important trade centre where merchants resided. There was busy traffic between the eastern and western wings of the Sātavāhana empire. (*Motichandrą* p.63, 64, 32 and *Yazadani* vol. I. p. 138 to 140).

May be on the account of wide spread network between ancient India and other countries, the common features like votive tanks are found in other countries also.

The votive tanks are found in Egypt; shrined models in the graves of Middle Empire; in Lemons; at Hephaestra; at Serpucia and at Rifeb.

The votice tanks may represent the universal flood and migration of flora and fauna to safer places. The tablet found from Nippur now present in the Pennynsylvania University, U.S.A. states that a storm swept the capital of Babylonia and destroyed mankind. Zisudru with some persons and animals rode out of the storm in a great boat and travelled to live in the sunrise land of Dilmuns.

According to tradition, Sumerian culture after chalcolithic age (4500-3100 B.C.) had been destroyed by a flood and pre and proto-historic period began with first Dynasty of Kish and Ur during 2900-2371 B.C.

Thus, flood, water destruction and saving the species from danger appears to have germ of truth. Perhaps when everything destroyed itslef in Sumer, cattle, birds and man might had been protected themselves from flood by transporting to some safe place like India as indicated from the votive tanks at chacolithic and megalithic sites of India. When everything normalised, animals, birds and people might had returned to their native places. The votive tanks found in different foreign countries and early historic site of India may indicate the flood theory. Thus the votive tanks indicate the trade, diśā-kāk as well as the flood-theory which was found in all ancient civilisations alongwith Indian evidences.

Places where votive tanks are found in India

1. Ahar, Ahad (27°42'; 75°38'). Dt. Udaipur (Rajasthan), about 3 km. east of Udaipur on the river Ahar, a tributary of the Banas.
2. Ahichchhtra, District Bareilly, (U.P.) the capital of North Panchala.
3. Arikamedu (11°55'; 79°50'), District Pondicherry, situated on the bank of a river formed into a lagoon barred by a sand-bar from the Bay of Bengal.
4. Bairat (27°27';76°12'), District Jaipur (Rajasthan), 66 kms. from Jaipur, situated on the hillock.
5. Bhir Mound near Taxila.
6. Bhita, District Allahabad (U.P.), about 22 km. up the Yamuna from Allahabad, on the right bank.
7. Bateswar (26°56'; 78°71') on the right bank of the Panchaganga.
9. Bhokardan, (20°16'; 46°47'), District Aurangabad, ancient Bhogavardhana, on the trade route from Ujjaiyini (Ujjain) to Pratisthana (Patthan).
10. Besanagar (23°32'; 77°48'), District Vidisha, ancient Vidisha nagara, a centre of cultural activities, with trade routes passing through it, on the banks of Betwa and Bes.
11. Chirand (25°45'; 84°50'), District Saran (Bihar) situated on the banks of Ghaghara, 11 kms. from Chhapra.
12. Chandoli (19°10';73°58'), District Pune (Mahārāshṭra), on the right bank of the river Ghod.
13. Devnimori (3°39';73°26'), District Sabarkantha, (Gujarat), the site is situated on the bank of Meshvo, a Buddhist site; now submerged.

14. Hastinapur (29°9';78°3'), District Meerut (U.P.). The site is located on the right bank of old bed of the Ganga; according to tradition it is the capital of Kauravas of the Mahābhārata time.
15. Kaundinyapura, (22°55';78°05'), District Amaravati (Maharashtra) located on the western bank of the Wardha, supposed to be the capital of the ancient Vidarbha. The birth place of and Rukmini, chief consort of Lord Krishna and that of epic and Damayanti.
15a. Kauśāmbī (25°20';81°23'), District Allahabad, 51.5 kms. s.-w. of Allahabad, on the bank of river Yamuna. The site spread over several villages; many highways, including some leading to the Deccan pass via Kauśāmbī. The site dates back to Chalcolithic cultures of central and western India and Harappa tradition; reveals PGW period II and III phases and NBPW in III and IVth a full developed Janapada style. Sanitary and waste-disposal arrangements is special feature of the site. Tanks, weep-holes, provision for seepage water; rampart alongwith moat and watch towers are noteworthy. The earliest habitation of the site dates back to 9th century B.C. The influence of Kushan and Saka-Parthian is noticed. The votive tanks are found in the early century of Christian era.
16. Kannauj (27°3';79°59'), District Farrukhabad, (U.P.). The ancient city of Kanyakubja situated on the southern bank of the Bhagirathi near the confluence of the Ganga and Kali.
17. Mathura (27°31';77°14'), District Mathura (U.P.). Situated on the banks of Yamuna is reputed as birth place of Krishna. Historically it is the capital of Kushans.
18. Masaon (25°10';2°25'), District Ghazipur, (U.P.).
19. Maheswar (22°11';75°36'), District West Nimar (M.P.). The twin sites on the northern and southern banks of the Narmada and on a slight bent of the river Narmada where it joins with Maheshwari. It is identified with

ancient city of Mahismati, the capital of Avanti which lay on the highway from Paithan to Ujjain.

20. Navadatoli see Maheshwar.
21. Nevasa (19°34';74°54'), District Ahmadnagar (Gujarat), situated on the both banks of Pravara.

21(a) Jhajjar, District Bhiwani (Haryana).

22. Nagari, District, Chittaurgarh, (Rajasthan), situated on the right bank of the Berach; identified with the Madhyamiki, the capital of Janapada of the Sibis.
23. Nagarjunakonda (16°31';79°14'), District Guntur (A.P.), ancient Vijayapuri situated on the right bank of Krishna, now submerged.
24. Paunar (20°47';78°41'), District Wardha (Maharashtra), located on the right bank of the river Dham, a tributary of the Wardha. It has been identified with ancient Pravarapura, the capital of the Vakatakas who ruled over Vidarbha.
25. Purānā Qilā (28°38';77°12'), New Delhi, situated on the bank of Yamuna, Delhi-Mathura-Agra road is identified with Indraprastha, the capital of Pandavas of Mahabaratha.
26. Rairh (26°20';76°10'), District Jaipur (Rajasthan) situated in the valley, surrounded with small hill ranges, located on isolated spur.
27. Rajghat (25°4';83°1'), District Varanasi (UP), on the northern outskirts of Varanasi city near the confluence of the Ganga and Barna (Varuna), the ancient city of the kingodom of Kasi, one of the 16 Mahājanapādas.
28. Rajgir (25°1';85°30'), District Nalanda (Bihar), situated in the valley completely enclosed with hills with two natural passes serving as gates. It is a naturally fortified area, served as capital Magadha which was later been a resort of Buddha and Mahavira, in the time of Ajatasatru.
29. Rangmahal (29°21';73°57'), District Ganganagar (Rajasthan), located in the dry bed of the Ghaggar

(Sarasvati), a typical ceramic industry with a distinct cultural trait is now called Rangmahal Culture.

30. Ram Nagar - See Ahichchhatra

31. Sanghol (30°48';76°12'), District Ludhiana (Punjab) situated on a dried-up course of the river Sutlej; a Buddhist stupa, monastaries, palace and etc. have been excavated.

32. Sambhar, District Jaipur (Rajasthan) an extensive mound on the bank of a dried-up lake representing ancient Sakambhari, the capital of the Imperial Chahamanas. It is near the Salt Lake.

33. Sirkap, now located in Pakistan.

34. Sonkh (27°29';77°31'), District Mathura (U.P.), 30 km. south-west of Mathura.

35. Shamalaji (23°41';73°26'), District Sabarkantha (Gujarat).

36. Sisupalgarh (20°13';85°51') (Orissa) the site sprawling on the south-east periphery of Bhubaneswar, has been indentified with ancient cities of Kalinga either Tosali or Kalinganagara.

37. Sankisa, District Farrukhabad(U.P.), situated on the bank of river Kalindi; is associated with the life of Buddha.

38. Surkotada (23°37';7050'), District Kochchh (Gujarat) brought to light the expansion of Harappan culture from Sind to Gujarat by land routes.

39. Taxila now situated in Pakistan.

40. Ter (18°20';76°10'), District Osmanabad (Maharashtra) identified with ancient Tagara, an important commercial centre famous for cloth.

41. Sopara : Sūrapāraka, the Capital of Aparantaka was an important city and Buddha site of Saka and Satavahana period.

42. Ujjain : (23°12';75°48'), headquarters of the District of the same name (Madhya Pradesh), situated on the

eastern bank of the river Sipra is well-known as capital of Avanti, one of the 16 mahājanapādas in the 6th century B.C. It was an important reglious and trade centre.

(This article was studied in the World Archaelogical Congress held from 4th to 10th December 1992)

References

1. Excavation at Ahar (Tomvata) (1961-62) by H.D. Sankalia, Decan College Post-Graduate and Research Inistitute, Poona (p.181-182).
2. Excavation at Devnimori (1960-63) by R.N. Mehta and S.N. Chaudhary, M.S. University, Baroda 1966 (p.90).
3. Excavation at Maheswar and Navadatoli (1952-53) by B. Subba Rao; S.B. Deo and H.D. Sankalia (Deccan College and Baroda University), Deccan College Research Institute Poona and M.S. University of Baroda - 1958. (p.197-198)
4. From History to Pre-history at Navasa (1954-56)by H.D. Sankalia, S.B.Deo, Z. Ansari, S.Ebrhadat Deccan College Post Graduate and Research Institute Poona - 1960 (p.381-82).
5. Excavation at Bhokardan (Bhogavardhana) 1973 by S.B. Deo, by Nagapur University and Marathwada University 1974 (p. 167-168-169).
6. Rang Mahal, the Swedish Archaeological Expedition to India - 1952-54 by Hanna Rydh, CWK Gleerup Publishers (Sweedan) - 1959.
7. Excavation at Syamalaji by Dr. R.N. Mehta and A.J. Patel, M.S. University of Baroda - 1967 (p.44).
8. Archaeological Remains and Excavation at Bairat by Rai Bhadur Daya Ram Sahani, Deptt. of Archaeology and Historical Research, Jaipur State - (1937) (p.31).
9. Report on the Excavations at Ter (1958), by B.N. Chapekar - 1969 (p 82-83)
10. Excavation at Rairh (1938-39, 39-40) by Dr. K.n. Puri, Deptt. of Archaeology and Historical Research, Jaipur State (p.44)
12. Taxila by Wheeler.
13. Ancient India vols 10,11,4.
14. Encyclopaedia of Archaeology, A. Ghosh Vols. I & II.
15. Archaeology of the Sātavāhana Kshatrapas by Dr. C. Margabandhu. Sandeep Prakashan New Delhi-1985 (pp 94-96)
16. Excavation at Kundinyapur by M.K. Dikshit, Director of Archives and Archacology; Maharashtra State-1968.

8

KATHĀVINÔDA

The inscriptions of the Western Chāḷukyans and those of the Kākatīyas of early medieval period (A.D. 957 to A.D. 1323) found in the Teleṅgāna region of Āndhra Pradesh[1] describe the ruling king as "Comfortably engaged in the entertainment of kathā" . However, what Kathāvinôda is not described anywhere in the inscriptions. The Mānasôllāsa of king Sômeśvara-III (A.D. 1126 - A.D. 1138) of the Western Chālukyan dynasty describes an entertainment entitled "Kathāvinôda" [2] as one of the recreation, enjoyed by a king. The same might had been referred to in the inscriptions.

The Mānasôllāsa describes Kathāvinôda as follows. After completing the daily duties of administration and law; enjoying food consisting of favourite items; the king, in a pleasent mood, should invite people who are expert in sixty four arts, four languagess and psychology; who are smart, alert, eloquent, matured, intelligent, youthful and capable; who are wordly wise, know well the truth (judgement), possess the discretion of time and place; are free from attachments (rāgadvēṣa); devoted to religion and righteousness; are capable of cutting the trees of misery with sword of detachment; who are highly detached from wordly affairs and are experts in the narration of different kathās in sriṅgāra and other sentiments and request to sing the kathās for him[3] and enjoy the Kathāvinôda.

On such occasion, the stories from Māhabhārata, Rāmāyaṇa, Purāṇas and Bṛihatkathās which are full of history and heroic acts; those which reflect worldy affairs, as well as the dramas and mahākāvyas which are full of beautiful descriptions, hyperboles; and the kathās of auspicious nature should be enjoyed by the king[4].

It is stated that the kathās are of four types (i) Ēkvatrika (ii) Dvivaṛika (iii) Chaturmukha (iv) Bahupuruṣa depending upon the number of singers engaged in each kathā, whether one, two, four or many[5]. In this connection, the characteristic features of different types of kathās and singers of kathās are described by Sômeśvara. The kathā sung by one whose voice is full of life; well-versed in all rāgas; eloquent; capable of reading the passages clearly; possess the knowledge of tāla (beat), gīta (lyric) and the kathā (story) which he sings and sings it with full of rasa (sentiment) and bhāva (emotion) is considered as the best Ēkavatrika. When two persons narrate the story of purāṇa imaginatively, it is called dvivatṛika.[6] A kathā sung by the sūta is prākṛit language, tuned to proper rāga and tāla; to the accompaniment of instruments of danḍaka and pataḥa; also accompanied by three female singers in melodious tunes at interval, is called chaturmukhī. When six singers sing or tell a kathā in Karṇāṭaka language, loudly and freely in the form of varṇa, in a fluid style, to the accompaniment of kinnarī and two mṛidangas, it is called bahupurusa kathā.

After giving styles of kathās, the pre-requisite qualities of singers of kathā are given by king Sômeśvara. It is stated that the one who knows the śabdaśāstra and well experienced in the worldy affairs; eloquent and reserved; who can explain the meaning of ślôka with sense, skillfull in telling the nature of the vēdas; who has worked hard in the field of literature and who has controlled his breath is called a good purāṇika. The person who knows different scripts and the nature of the lyrics; possess good and melodious voice and can read a verse according to pada (word) and chandas (meter) with good tune is considered as the best vāchika. The one who can imagine and knows well the stories of purāṇas is called *Dvivatṛka*.[7]

Besides the heroic deeds and noble history of the age old kings, the sacred acts and sacrifices made were sung as kathās in various bhāvas and rasas for the king. At times, the king himself sings love songs of vipralaṁbha and poems on his lovers[8].

Sauryôdārya guṇôpētā dādbutarasāśrayā (1428) //
raudra vībhaṭsa hāsya dvā karuṇô bhayānirbharā
sṛingāra rasa saṁpūrṇa prēmabhôgasu saṁbhṛita //
vipralaṁbha rasôpētēna darghatī ghaṭanānvita
īrṣa darpa samāpēta mada môḥa samanvita //
nāna svyachati trā ḍhya nṛipachitta pramôdinī
ākarṇa yôtkadhāḥ śravyo divyā bhāva manoharaḥ//
svayam cha kathā yôdrājā prēyasī prēmavrittayô
evaṁ kathā vinôdayaṁ sravyāṇāṅdakarôvarāḥ //

Thus, the king enjoys his liesure time listening to different types of kathās and himself singing at times.[9]

The above given qualification to be possessed by the singers, the nature and composition of kathās[10] and the reference to the terms śabda, tāla, gīta with special reference to the 64 kaḷās, rasas, bhāvas and psychology throw light on the contemporary theory of aesthetics[10-A].

The origin of aesthetics in India may be traced back to vēdic period with special reference to Upaniṣads. But Bharata's Nāṭya Śāstra is the earliest and systematic treatise on aesthetics with special reference to audio-visualal arts. To begin with the topic, traditional proposition of kaḷās in the concept of chatuśaṣṭikala had influenced king Sômeśvara as he also referred to kaḷās as sixty-four in numbers.

In the context to the 'Bhāva', 'Rasa' and number of rasas a brief backdrop on Indian aesthetics is given here.

Bhāva : According to Nātya Śāstra, that which is bhavita/pervaded is bhāva (emotional ferver or mental state); in other way that which makes the idea through words, gesticulation, temperamental representation, and produce/stimulates rasa is called bhāva[11].

The Bhavas are (i) sthāyī (permanently dominant or basic emotions); (ii) sañcārī (moving or transitory emotions); and (iii) sāttvika (temperamental or originated from mind). The sthāyī bhāvas are innate in character. Every creature is endowed with bhāvas which are eight in number e.g. rati (love), hāsya (merriment) and like. The sancārī bhāvas are thirty-three in number like nirvēda (despendency); and these promote or develop the sthāyībhāvas and transform into Rasa, like waves in the sea etc. The sāttvika bhāvas (voluntary emotions) are infallible signs of emotions; eight in number, revealed in physical forms like stambha (paralysis), svēda (sweat) and etc. Thus, altogether there are forty-nine bhāvas which cause the manifestation of rasa[12]. These bhāvas are relished as rasa when properly developed by vibhāvas and anubhāvas.

Vibhāvas : (Hētu or casue / emotive situation) : It is special knowledge known or determined; hence it is called vibhāva (determinent). Vibhāva has two aspects (i) alaṁbana—the object primarily responsible for the arouse of emotions; and (ii) uddīpana - the environment which enhances the emotion[13].

Anubhāva : The bhāva is made to be felt, hence it is called anubhāva (consequent or expression); the physical changes which are consequent on the rise of emotions are called anubhāvas[14]. The anubhāvas and vibhāvas are to be known or understood by means of abhinaya. These co-exist with sub-consicious emotional dispostiion (vāsanas) of the spectator/reader and make him to experience an identical emotion with the actor/author[14-A].

The sthāyībhāvas surrounded by (in combination with)

vibhāvas (determinents) and anubhāvas (expression) together with vyabhicārībhāvas (transitory states) produce/ evoke rasa (relish) with aesthetic object, to the consciousness.

Vibhāvānubhāva-vybhicāri-symyôgad-rasnispattiḥ" [15]

Sage Bharata recognised four basic rasas i.e. sṛiṅgāra, raudra, vīra and vībhatsa and states that hāsya originates from sṛiṅgāra; karuṇā (pathetic) from raudra (furious); adbhuta (marvellous) from vīra (heoric) and bhayānaka (terrible) from vībhatsa (odious)[16]. According to Nāṭya śāstra each rasa has its own presiding deity and colour[17]. It is stated that each aesthetic emotion (rasa) is based on a particular emotional disposition. Thus the eight permanent classes of basic emotions (sthāyībhāvas) and eight rasas are the natural correlation of each other namely sṛiṅgāra (the erotic), hāsya (humourous), karuṇā (pathos), raudra (impetvious anger), vīra (heroic), bhayānaka (terrific), vībhatsa (odious) and adbhuta (mysterious) evokes bhāvas (permanently dominent) viz. rati (love), hāsya (merriment), śôka (sorrow), krôdha (furry), utsāha (enthusiasm), bhaya (terror), jugupsā (disgust), and vismaya (astonishment)[18].

However, these become accessory states (vyabhicāri-hāvas) of those aesthetic sentiments which are not their natural correlate, but helps to intense them e.g. mirth is necessary to feed sentiment of erotic, anger for herioc sentiment and like that[19].

As already seen, the basic emotion (stāyībhāva), the excitement (uddīpanavibhāva), the mental state disposition (bhāva), the transitory emotions (sañacārībhāvas), and expression of emotion exhibited (sāttvika bhāvas), arose an aesthetic emotion or rasa e.g. the erotic sentiment (sṛiṅgāra) has love (rati) for its permanent emotional disposition (sthāyībhāva); the beloved person for its determent cause (ālambana vibhāva); garlands, sandal paste, etc. for its excitement cause (uddīpana vibhāva); and casting glances etc. for its transitory emotion (vyabhacārībhāva)[20]. Sriṅgāra again is divided into vipralaṁbha and samyôga.

All the above said 49 bhāvas except ālasya (lethargity), krôdha (feriocity) and jugupsā (disgust) further could be developed as sṛiṅgāra[21].

While narrating the rasas, the erotic sentiment is treated first, because its basic permanent emotional disposition rati (instinct of love or personal delight in an object or a desire) is common to all creatures and is agreeable to all. The comic sentiment is treated next because it is principally directed towards an object (artha)[22].

Dhanañjaya (1000 A.D.) in his Daśarūpaka, a commentary on Bharata's Nāṭya śāstra, mentions that an aesthetic enjoyment or relish springs from the bliss of the self, owing to the appreciation of the meaning of poetry or drama.

"Svādaḥ kāvyārtha saṁbēdadātmānaṅda - samudhavaḥ"

He holds that the rise of the basic mental state is due to the contextual power of language (tātparya) and that the universalisation of the subjective and objective aspect of the aesthetic experience, due to the powers of the poetic and dramatic composition.[23] When the permanent emotional disposition or sub-conscious vāsana is aroused to consciousness and transforms into rasa, it vibrates over strings of the heart of the spectator and pervades the physical body. Accordingly, "The emotions of (emotion is the actual process which comes out as conscious) erotic and emotion of the ludicrous bring about blooming or unfolding (vikāśa) of consciousness. The heroic emotion and the emotion of wonder generate expansion (vistāra) of consciousness. The emotion of horror and fear produce kṣhôbha. The emotion of fury and pathos bring about obstructions (vikṣēpa) of consciousness. Here, the mental vikāśa is compared to that of flower's bloom and vistāra to the spreading of the branches of a tree while kṣhôbha is compared to the agitation of the ocean and vikṣepa to the obstruction lying in the path of the strong wind".[24]

Abhinava Gupta (1200 A.D.) who wrote on extensive commentary on Nāṭya śāstra mentions that the aesthetic of erotic sentiment (sṛiṅgāra rasa) is the only rasa; it is similar to the intutive experience of Brāhman, which creates an extraordinary wonder (alaukikachamatkārakari). It is devoid of consciousness of any other object; when revived and manifested rasa enters the heart and permeates the whole organism and is experienced. However, he laid importance on the Dhvani aspect of the poetry.[25]

Thus the aesthetic enjoyment involves subconscious and conscious psychological process, where the 'natural urges of man seem to have been sublimited into normative values'. [25-A]

Basically, all beings have an instinct or tendency (vṛitti) towards happiness (aṇanda). However, on being discontented in their disposition, the sense organs introvert and try to discover the asesthetic relish in the inner self or pure conciousness or antaḥkaraṇa and reach aesthetic elightment by the practice of concentration and meditation.[26] As per the philosophy of Sāṅkhya-yôga which form the substratum of all aesthetic theories, the psyco-physical activities are due to the predominance of Rajas aspect of prakṛiti, the Eternal matter. Once the self introverts, the pure Sāttivika nature dominates Rajas and Tāmas, and the aesthetic relish is awakened, the pure consciousness (the self) culminates in philosophical contemplation, identifying Ātma with Paramātma. [27]

"Vibhāvādi-sādhāranīkaranātmanā-bhāvakatva-vyāpārēna
bhāvyamānaḥ sthāyī sattvôdrēka-prakāśānanadamaya-
saṁvid-viśrānti-satattvena bhôgēna bhujyate iti
bhaṭṭanāyakaḥ"

Coming to the number of rasas mentioned in

Mānasôllāsa, it is clear that the concept of eight rasas propounded by Bharata and his followers Dhañanjaya and Sāradātanaya (12 century A.D.) had influenced king Sômeśvara unlike that of Abhinava Gupta (12 century A.D.) who propounded the theory of Nava rasas including śānta rasa (quiteness). [27a]

Further, king Sômeśvara treated the Kathāvinôda as an independent entertainment. Though, he allotted separate chapters to literature, dance, vocal and instrumental music did not deal with drama as vinôda separately. Perhaps the Kathāvinôda in which the songs set to music is enjoyed, might be a form of druva songs, an important feature of drama.

Since by means of aesthetic enjoyment, human beingss are supposed to rise from matter to spirit, Sage Bharata, categorically laid down the qualification of the artists, singers, instrumentalist and acharyas as well as the method of application of the gīta and rasa in art form. The description of the singers narrated above by king Sômeśvara tally with the norms laid down by Sage Bharata. [28]

Thus, so far as the nature of aesthetic experiences, number of rasas, character of singers, the purpose of art are concerned, Mānasôllāsa reveals the influence of Bharata and his successors Dhananjaya and Saradatanaya.

(This article was read in XVIIth session of Āndhra Pradesh History Congress 1992.)

References

1. Inscriptions of Warangal District, Āndhra Pradesh, Archaeological Series, Govt. of Āndhra Pradesh, Hyderabad, pp. 48, 57, 61, 118 and 147.
2. *Mānasôllāsas of king Bhūlôkamalla Sômēśwara*, Volume-III, Gaekwad's Oriental Series, Vadodara, 1961.
3. *Ibid*, 4.19, V.No. 1406-1411.
4. *Ibid* V.No. 1414-1417.
5. *Ibid*, V.No. 1412-1417.
6. *Ibid*, V.No. 1419-28.

7. *Ibid.*
8. *Ibid.*
9. *Ibid.*
10. *Ibid*, V.No. 1430-32.
10a. Aesthetics is science and philosophy of art. The term is derived from Greek word 'Aisthesies' - sense perception. The work of art, human behaviour towards art, psycho analysis, history of art, standard used for criticism and evolution of art, functions of art, values of art, aesthetic experience, configuration involved in aesthetic experience are some of the aspects discussed under aesthetics.
11. Translated by a Board of Scholars—*The Nāṭya Śāstra* (N.S) Rāga Natya Series No. 2, Sri Satguru publications, New Delhi, Chp. 7, prose passage before V.No. 1-3; Dr. K.C. Pandey, *Comparative Aesthetics*, Vol. I, pps. 12-21 Chaukhamba Sanskrit series studies Vol. II, 1950.
12. N.S. Chapter 7, V.No. 7 and the prose passage before it; N.S. Chapter, 6, V.No. 17-20; *Agnipurāṇa*, pp. 1244-1247 edited by Manmath Datt, Vol.II, Calcutta.
13. N.S. Chap. 7, prose passage and V.No. 4; Dr. R.C. Pandey Vol.I, pp. 16-17 and *Agnipurāṇa*, p. 1247.
14. N.S. Chapter No. 6, prose passage after V.No. 31 and chapter 7, V.No.6, prose passage after 4; Dr. Pandey Vol. I, pp. 16-17.
14a. N.S. Chapter No. 7, V.No. 6; Jha, p.170.
15. N.S. Chapter 6, V.No. 3-38, prose passage after V.No. 31 and chapter 7, prose and passage after V.No. 7.
16. N.S. Chapter No. 6, V.No. 39-41; *Agnipurāṇa*, p. 1244.
17. N.S. Chapter 6, V. No. 42-45.
18. N.S. Chapter 6, V. No. 15 and 17.
19. N.S. Chapter, 67
    and Jadunath Sinha's– *Indian Psychology Vol. II "Emotion and Will"*, p. 287, Moti Lal Banarasi Das 1986.
20. N.S. Chapter 7, V. No. 7, prose passage after V. No. 8 and Jha, p. 289-30.
21. N.S. Chapter 7, V. No. 107.
22. N.S. Chapter 6, V. No. 39-41 and Chapter 7, V. No. 9; Jha p. 288; The Agni Purāṇa States that the absolute consciousness however dawns upon the soul or consciousness of man, and pervades through the essence of ego. Out of egoism, proceeds attachment which become strong in course of time and ultimately developes into the sentiment of love. Different sentiments thus originate from different attributes of the soul; in other way the sentiments are divine in nature.
23. Dr. Pandey, p. 177-78, Jha, p. 165.

24. Jha p. 169 and Pandey p. 127; Descrates (1596-1650 AD) a Western philosopher states that the aesthetics is an intellectual joy accompanied by emotion; and he explains the mechanism of physiology and biology of each emotion. The Upaniṣadic concept of Panchakôśa and Panchaprāṇas also may be studied in this context.
25. Jha p.172-73, Mammata Bhatta states that sentiment is aroused to consciousness through the activity (vyāpāra) called revival (bhāvaktva), with which the spectator identifies himself with poet, transforms into rasa and enjoyes the blissful experience due to dominance of Sattva. It is like experience of self as pure consciousness. Bhôjrāja of later period also believed that sṛiṅagāra is the main sentiment of aesthetic taste. "Sṛingāraekaivarasa" . This is akin to the theory of western psycologist FREUD, who feels that aesthetic taste is the medium of sex satisfaction.
25a. The introduction by R.N. Dandekar to Dr. Padma Sudhi's *Aaesthic theories of India.*
26. Dr. Padma Sudhi–*Aesthetic theories of India;* Bhandarkar oriental series No. 18, Bhandarkar Oriental Research Institute, Poona, 1983, pp. 5-6, p. 19 and p.48. 'According to FREUD Kama when is enjoyed with satisfaction, becomes beauty. But when it becomes dissatisfied, it eradicates itself from the feeling and moves to sublimate into a philosophy of art; see the theory of Mamatta Bhatta Bharata, Sāradātanaya, Guna Chandra, Ramachandra and others on Rati & Jha, pp. 177-184.
27. Pandey, Vol., P. 128-130 and Vol. II, p. 120-212, *Padma Sudhi,* pp. 96-104 & Jha, p. 172.
27a. Pandey, pp. 176-177 & 184-194; Jha, p. 308.
28. N.S., Chapter, 32, V.N. 494-98, 503-511 & 512-574.

9

VAJRALĒPA

Every human being is inherently sensitive to his surroundings and reacts to whatever he looks at. He expresses or communicate his reactions and feelings voluntarily or involuntarily in the form of shape and colour which in other way is called an art. The earliest man expressed his observations on the nature and experiences of life perhaps even his desires, in the form of drawing/ paintings in prehistoric caves or rockshelters of Kaimur range of Central India; Raigarh, Mirzapur range of U.P., and in caves sprawling in Rajasthan, Orissa, Tamilnadu, Āndhra Pradesh, Karnataka and Kerala, which formed his dwellings. The paintings were made on the surface of plain rock; representing the themes of huntings, singing, dancing as well as his natural surroundings. Man thus tried to arrest the fleeting thoughts and objects of beauty in a permanent form.

In course of time, rise of powerfull kingdoms resulted in the prolification of structural buildings by using the materials like mud, brick, rock and wood. Thus by 4th to 6th centuries of christian era, a technique of building construction and unique method of preparation of ground for painting was developed. Though, the practice of painting on the wall of rock caves continued till the times of the Guptās, Pallavās, Chāḷukyas of Bādāmī, Rāṣhṭrakūṭas and the Chôlas, the advent of structural temples was commissioned even before the times of Guptās in the North; by the Sātavāhan and (2nd B.C.) Pallavās in the South and the Chāḷukyas (5th A.D.) in the Decan simultaneously. Thus necessity of innovation of cement or binding material arose specially in case where the paintings are to be executed. At this juncture, India has witnessed a renaissance in all walks of cultural life. Apart from the āgamic literature, cannons like Brihatsaṁhitā (Chap 57) Viṣṇudharmôttarapurāṇa (Chap 92) Īśānguru paddhati (Chap 47) and other were composed on technical topis like architecture, sculpture, iconography and paintings. The technique "Vajralēpa" is unique in the history of Indian paintings.[1]

In connection with "Vajralēpa" the topic under study, the Viṣṇudharmôttarapurāṇa (5-7 A.D.) refers it as binding material and gives different methods of preparation of this binding material based on the vegetable, animal and mineral sources[2]. The Bṛihatsaṁhitā refers to an adament based on vegetables as vajralēpa; the adament based salts as vajrasaṅghaṭa. While referring the uses of the above adaments, Bṛihasaṁhita states that vajralēpa as binding material for buildings, temples, palaces, walls, wells and fixing the images but does not refer to the use of other types of adaments in a specific terms[3]. Shri M.C. Joshi expressed that vajrasaṅghāṭa might have been used for mending the metallic objects[4] as suggested by Maya.

The Chāḷukyas of Kalyāṇī who ruled over present Karnataka and Āndhra during 11th - 12th centuries were great patrons of the painting besides architectures. The temple of Kôlpāka, Paccalasômēswera, Allahdurgh are some of the silent witness of their love for art. King Sômēśwara III son of Vikramāditya IV, gives a detailed account on painting in Mānasôllāsa composed by him in A.D. 1129-A.D. 1130 and the term vajralēpa is used by king Sômēśwara in connection with the preparation of the ground for the painting[5].

It is stated that at first instance, the wall where the painting is proposed to be executed should be white-washed and kept devoid of cracks, breaks as well strains or blots; then the lepana is to be applied equally and evenly. At this point kind Sômēśwara gives the method of preparation of the *lēpana* as follows

The skin of buffallo is cooked in milk till it becomes a soft paste like butter. This lepana is to be rubbed with pressure when it is dried becomes hard. This is called vajralepa and is the best fitted always for the purpose of paintings. This is to be kept on sticks, which are again kept in a boiled water in earthern pot. When it is ready, a little of the lēpana is mixed within different colours with specific quantity in order to get the desirable shade of the colour; so that the colour of the paintings will not scale off. Further, the swēta mrittikā (white clay) is mixed with vajralēpa and coated well smoothly and evenly on the wall three times for the purpose of paintings. So also the powder of counch and soft sand are to be mixed and rubbed well (furnished), till the wall is equal, even, smooth and bright. Besides, a dhātu called nāga which is white like moon available in the hills of Nilgiri is also to be mixed with vajralepa, stirred well (pulvarised) and applied on the wall with palm delicately, slowly and freely. on the wall prepared thus, an intelligent painter should draw the outline of the pictures, decorate with tasteful colour scheme full of rasas" . Thus, The vajralēpa is used for preparation of the ground as well as binding materials to the colours. This is the technique of tempera given by king Sômēśvara.

As suggested by Stella Kramrisch Vajralēpa was intended for external application several times on a thin coats of lime plaster for the preparation of a ground for paintings[6].

However, generally scholars/writers on ancient Indian

painting feel that the methods of preparation of ground and colour or technique of paintings given in the ancient texts are just imaginative; were not given by real artists, and that they are not proved to be correct and never tally with the chemical analysis. It is even stated that vajralēpa referred to in the texts was never used/applied practically[7].

Therefore, the chemistry of the leather/skin which constitutes the basic material of the vajralēpa according to Mānasôllāsa is given here[8].

When the animal skin or bone is boiled in water for some time, the connective tissues of the skin which have collagen finally dissolve in water. This product is called glue. In order to use the glue for painting purpose first the glue is soaked in cold water to swell, then heated in water bath to dissolve it, this hot syrup should be kept in hot water bath. When the glue dries, many cracks appear on the painting or on the ground due to contractions. Therefore, preservatives should be added to the glue.

Thus, the preparation and use of glue given even in the present day texts is the same as given by Sômēśwara in Mānasôllāsa.

Since the glue is hygroscopic, it expands in high humidity and contracts in dry environment and swells in cold water; the formaldehyde is used as preservative from observing water. Casein the main protein in the milk acts as collodial solution. It swelss in water but does not dissolve. So in order to make it useful as medium for painting, first casein should be dissolved in lime and the resulting substance is called cold glue. It has a good properties. Once dried, casein becomes a water resistant. That is why materials like lime, counch powder svetamrittikā and milk might have been recommended by Sômēswara for the preparation of Vajralēpa.

Casein works as a good medium for the paintings or colours which are alkaline resistance. That is, a painting medium made of casein and lime is most durable for wall painting and dry walls.

Besides, tempera binding media consists acqueous phase, the non-acqueous phase and an amulsifier. In case of casein since it is a colloid state works as a good emulsifier. Perhaps that is the reason why Sômēśwara prescribed milk to be used while cooking the skin of buffallo in the preparation of vajralēpa.

Thus, the vajralēpa referred to in Mānasôllāsa is not just theory or imagination as felt by some scholars, but it is a reality applied in the execution of the paintings of that period,which are still available[9].

The use of skin or leather and milk in the art of painting has been found in other countries like Egypt, Rome, etc[9] and even in modern period.

(This article has been read in Āndhra Pradesh Historical Conference held at Hyderabad in 1998.)

References

1. *Journal of Rock Art Painting.*
2. *Shri Viṣṇudharmottara* by Dr. Priyabala Shah The New Order Book Co. Ahmedabad, 1990.
3. *Varāhamihira's Brahat Saṁhitā*-PT. I by Prof. M. Ramakrishna Bhat, Motilal Banarsidass, Delhi 1981.
4. Vajralēpa and its use and Shri M.C. Joshi:
5. *Mānasôllāsa* by Bhūlôkamalla Sômēśvara, Gaekwad's Oriental Series, No. Baroda, 1939 Vimsali III 13-V; No.132040.
6. The Hindu Temple by Stella Kramrisch PP 121-129 F.N.N. of P. 122.
7. *Techniques in Indian Mural Painting* by Jayanta Chakrabarti, K.P. Bagchi & Company, Calcutta, 1980 (17 & 24) Classical Painting Vidya Bhavan in III P 545-47.
8. UNESCO Mannual on conservation.
9. During the discussion in the session of Āndhra Historical conference held from 10th-12th January, 1998 in Hyderabad, the officer of Chemistry Branch, Deptt. of Archaeology and Museum, Government of Āndhra Pradesh stated that the Western Chāḷukyan painting from Kôlanupāka, Āndhra Pradesh revealed the traces of Vajralēpa.

10

MUSICAL PILLARS An Unique Feature of Vijaya-Nagara Architecture

The Vijayanagara dynasty which swayed its power over a major portion of the sub-continent had expressed its vigour in art, architecture and culture too. The tall gôpuras, long manḍapas, gigantic pillars with complex designs are some of the morvels of Vijayanagara civil engineering. Of all, the pillars are the most interesting.

Generally the temples are honoured with gôpuras on cardinal directions or on two sides, or on front side only. The manḍapas were raised in relation to complex rituals and festivals; and pillars in numerous composite forms were erected to carry the magnificient verandahs and manḍapas like nāṭyamanḍapa, kalyāṇamanḍapa and other types. These pillars are of various types : pillar with (a) rearing horse, (b) portrait, (c) rempart hipograph, (d) miniature shrine; (e) with shaft 8-18 sides (f) with ornamental bracket and hanging bud, (g) with nagabandha, (h) kumbhapanjara, (i) motif of ornamental scrolls and (k) the so called musical pillars. These musical pillars are carved with a strong central core and number of small side pillars around. Each small pillar porduces musical note when tapped delicately. An attempt is made here to study the scriptural and scientific basis for vastu of musical pillars.

What is music? When any object or organ is thrown into state of vibrations by some agency, vibrations spread to the surrounding air and these impinge upon eardrum and set up a nervous disturbance to the mind which we call sound. The pitch of sound depends upon the frequency of vibrations of the original sound prodcucing body. Any particular body capable of being set in vibration has its natural frequency of vibration depending on the size, density and tension. The lenght of the subject also determines pitch. The transition tones and antindent notes give rise to overtones or Hormonis. Thus, on account of one body by striking another one causes an agitation which is called vibrations or resonence and the continuous vibrations of equal lenght of the sound waves is called music. While the frequency of the vibrations determines the pitch, the amplitude of vibrations determines the loudness.

Thus, some stones/pillars when tapped or struck with metal piece, wooden piece, or even by hand give rise to different hormonies, giving the effect of music. The lithophone (Litho-stone, phone-sound) thus, is a percussion instrument made of stone.

Sands the deserts of Arabia and libya boom or wail with the wind or when stirred with a rod; or when blown upon by the breeze produce music. This is the lithophone made by nature. Now, the lithophons made by men are described.

The role of the pillar (stambha)in the Indian architecture is very vital. It regulates the whole structure, as well as supports the roof; bearing the stress and transmits the load to the soil; and gives elevation to the building. Depending upon the nature of the building, its height and width as well as number of the storys, the number of stambhas and their disposition and shape are planned by the architect.

The Matsyapurāṇa, Maya śāstra, Mānasāra, Viśwakarma vāstu and Kāsyapaśilpa specially describe pillar and its, varities.

According to Viśvakarma Vāstu, the stambhas are of 6 kinds depending upon the number of faces. The pillar which is cylinderical is called Dēvankānta stambha. That of 4 faces is called Brahmakānta; of 6 faces Indrakanta; of 8 faces Viṣnukānta; of 12 faces Skandakranta and of 16 faces Sômakānta. Designs of flowers and figures also can be chiselled in parts of the pillar for which purpose the necessary part is shaped with four faces only. The upapītha or the pedestal of pillar is carved as the lowest part of the pillar and the architrave is placed above the pillar and below the roof firmly. Pillars which have sides or additions of smaller pillars 1, 2, 3, 4 or more in number are classified into six types, Supratikānta, Sūryakānta Brahmakānta, Kailāsakānta, Mērukānta and Nadikānta. The Nandikānta type of pillar is the prototype of the musical pillar.

The sound of the musical tones produced are like that of the jalatarangam cups. In some cases the notes are as bright and clear as those of metal gongs, mṛidaṅga or ḍamaru, dôlu, tabla, cymbols, jēghaṅṭa and ghaṭam. The colour of the stone pillars is white, grey or black or even of sandalwood. The height of the pillar range form three to six feet. These pillars have no ornamental base or decorated floral top; support the roof like the other ordinary pillars. These are invariably found along the sides of the temple halls, or courtyards; along the periphery, with the residual central massive pillars serving to give stability to the entire structure.

Why only the lithophone pillars produce music but not all stones? Let us see the ancient texts in this regard.

The petrological study made by the ancient Indian sages is very interesting. Almost all texts on vastu or temple worship devote a chapter on the selection of the stone for the buildings with special reference to the temples.

Regarding the sources of stone, the Vāyupurāṇa gives at a length the description of the mountains from which good stone can be obtained. The Visvakṣēna saṁitha and the Hayaśīrṣa paṅcharātra state that the stone can be obtained from mountain or from earth. But the Nārada saṁhita refers to mountain only as source of good stone. Some texts like Hayasīrṣa and Visvakṣēna divide the lands form which the stone is available into four types. i.e. mahēndri, vāyuvi, agnēya and varuṇi. The former text further states that the mahēndri is available in Madhyadēśa, the vāyuvi in Marudēśm; the agnēya in Ghūrjaradēśa and varuni in Anūpadēśa. But the Sanatkumārasaṁhitha states that the agnēya stone called Sāṅkari, is hot, so should be avoided. The Sanathkumāra Saṁhita gives another division of the stone as anulôma and prathilôma of which former variety is to be selected.

All these texts give detailed directions regarding the places to be searched as well the places to be avoided for selection of the best stone.

The Viṣhu Dharmôttara, Aparājithapṛichchā and Ajithāgama refer to three vimalas (defects of the stone) namely kāṅsaya, hēma and lôha . It is stated that the stone which contains ironore, reduces population; that which contians bronzeore destroys the honour of the people, and that full of gold ore brings famine and destruction.

All these ancient texts state that, when polished, if stone reveals circular lines or cuts should be known as the "Sagarbha" (one with some creatures in it). If the stone has an extremely red colour as manjisth (red as madder) then, there is a frog in it. If circular lines of yellow colour are oberved, one should know that a godha (a big lizard) lives in it; and if black ones are, a serpent and if tawny, a rat.

According to engineering geology of modern period, the stability and durabiliy of the building stone and its minerological composition are important. For building purpose, the stone should be unshatterd, cut into a whole mass; cleavage should be clear; it should slip freely and slide forward byits own weight.

The best stone can be obtained from selected cliffs or along with streams. The building stone should be free from cracks; have uniform texture, attractive colour; banding, capable of taking polish, stong, hard and sound; free from algee, lichen, effloresence and devoid of porocity and cappillary action. The stone should be free from minerals like mica and gneiss. The oldest rock or igneous granite is good for building. The building stone should have uniform, fine granular texture as it gives strength to the stone; and it should have property of low obsorption; Crushing strength, fire resistance, weather resistant; good in looks and have good fracture i.e. the stone should be glossy so that it could break with good conchoidal fracture. Thus, both anscient texts and modern science give the same directions in regard to the best stone.

According to the ancient texts, a stone is said to be 'male' when it is of uniform colour, dense, smooth and perfectly cylinderical and when it gives off the sound of an elephant bell. A 'female' stone has a wide bottom and a narrow head and gives off the sound of a cymbol. A 'neuter'stone has narrow top and bottom, a wide median part and gives off no sound. Stone again is divided into three classes, 'young', 'mature' and 'aged'. A 'young' stone is soft when struck by an implement such as a hatchet, gives off a sound similar to that of a partly baked brick. A 'mature'stone is smooth and round; and gives off a deep sound; cold and sweet; is not fragmented and glows. This stone 'in the prime of life' is suitable for every sort of use and contributes to the success of all work.

According to the principles of petrology (science of rocks) the rock forms the unity of earth's crust; it goes about 10 miles in depth. The first solid material is called magma. The primary magma is generally called igneous rock and then it is attacked by water and wind on account of which hollows are formed and filled with minerals, tree and organic remains, the stone is called sedimentary rock or secondary rock. In course of time these primary and, secondary rocks under changes due to earth movements pressure and heat produced. According to Petrology the igneous rock is acidic due to presence of silicon and allumia; and sedimentory is basic due to occurrence of iron oxide and magnesia. So also metals like nickel, platinum are found in periodotiles.

The ancient texts direct that the "Sagarbhasila" should not be used and gives the evil effects of such sila.

The Modern science, too says that sedimentary stone can be identified by the frequent occurance of organic materials like fossils of land and sea or shallow water deposition. The shelly line stone contains the marine organic deposits; guano contains the fish eating sea birds; in the oolite the iron bacteria is noticed, so also coral are some living organisms in the stone. The coal peat is formed due to the accumulation of the plant debris,metamorphysed due to heat, pressure and thrust.

The Śhilparatna,Vishnudharmôttra, Aparājithapṛichcha and other texts give general colours of the stone and good and bad effects.

According to modern science the colour of the stone depends upon the minerals present in it. The colour of the granite depends upon the colour of the felsper, one of the main components.

The āgmas and the purāunās bive directions that white stone should be taken (to represent the god) as this being suitable brāhmins. For kṣhatriya the colour of stone should be red; for vaiśyās yellow and for sūdra black. The stone should be of uniform colour and should be dense, smooth an deeply embeded in the earth, under the shade of a tree or by the side of a river water; massive, smooth, uniform in colour; be of appropriate length and width and not effected by blazing sun or fire; too soft; that which has been in alkaline water; which is shaky and which has been displaced, rough or already been used; the stone with streaks, spots or flaws and aged, cross grained should be avoided; stone which contains grit; which is of indefinite colour; one with cracks; gives off no sound; which is alveolar, fissured or pregnant should not be used.

Coming to sound aspect of petrological study, the ancient texts use the terms "kāṅsyagaṅṭa" or "kāṅsyatāḷa", "tīvragaṁbhīra" or "madhura", "gaṅṭānishwana", tālaśabda; "mandadvani" "suswara". The Rūpamaṅḍana refers to "ajaghanṭāswara" while Maya used the word gaja ghaṅṭārava in reference to the good sound of a stone. The Kāśypiya states that a stone is classified according to the sound it produces. When the sound of kāṅsya, in short duration is produced, when struck, the stone is Bāla; when the stone gives ghanṭādhavani, for a long time, it is called youth; further, the sound of ghanṭa for a long time in deep pitch is produced by a male stone, but the sound like tāḷa in a long duration is produced by female stone: The Ajithāgama even describes the letters that can be heard by tapping the stone.

According to modern petrology, large crystals of quartz and felspar are found in granite and on account of this, stone is used in the ceramic industry. The granodiorate also is composed of quartz and felspar. Perhaps this aspect of granite and similar stones which makes them to produce sound was exploited by the ancient sages and architects for building the musical pillars in the temples and used in religious worship while for singing and dancing.

The granodiorate and granite gneises are plenty in the old archean rocks of India and these-were used in building temples in ancient period, where the musical pilhar formed very important part of the temple.

[This article was read in the National Seminar on Vijayanagara Empire at Hyderabad in 1999]

BIBLIOGRAPHY

Agitagama by N.R. Bhatt, Pondicherry- 1964

Aparājita Prichchha Ed. by Propatbhai Ambashankar Mankad Pub. by Oriental Institute Vadodara-1950

Administrative & Social life under Vijayanagar by T.V Mahalingam Madras University-1975

A Descriptive Bibliography of Printed texts of *Panchratragamas* Vol. I Pub. by Oriental Institute of Vadodara-1975.

Conservation of building and decotive stone Vol. I Ed. by John Asburst and Francies G. Dimes Pub. by Heimeman, London-1990

Hayasīrṣa Pancharatra, Pub. by Varandra Research Society, Rajasthan-1956

Indian Archectura—Percy Brown

Jayakhya Samhita, Ed. by Krishama Charya

Kāsyapiya Samhita, Ed. by VG. Apte Pub. by Anand Ashram-1926

Mayamata and many more. Ed. by Ganapati Sastri, Pub. by Trivanduram Sanskrit Series

Music Through the Ages, Ed. by V. Premalatha, Pub. by Sundeep Prakashan, Delhi-1985.

Musical Engineering, Ed, by Harry F. Olson, Pub. by McGraw-Hill Book Company, Inc. New York 1952-53.

Nāradīya Samhita, Ed. by Rai Sheva Prasad Choudhry, Pub. by Kendriya Sanskrit Vidyapeeth, Tirupati-1971

Padma Saṁhita

Physics Pt. I, Ed. by Robert Research and David Halldy Pub. by Willey Eastern Ltd. 1979.

Principles of petrology

Rūpa-Manḍana of Mandana Sūtradhāra, Ed. by Upendra Mohan, Pub. by Sankhyarirtha

Srirasnasamihita, Ed. by Ms. Seeta Padrachhar, Pub. by Kendriya Sanskrit Vidypeeth, Tirupati-1963

Sanatkumarainhita, Pandit V Krinamacharya, Pub. by Adeyar Library & Research Centre-1969

Śilpa-Ratna, Ed. by Srikumara, Pub. by Trivandrum Sanskrit Series

Samarāṅga Sūtradhāra by Bhoja, Ed. by T. Ganapati Shastri, Pub. by Gaekwad Sanskrit Series-1966

Sri Vishnu Dharmôttara, Trs.by Dr. Priyabaia Shah, Allahabad

Selected Temples of Rayalaseema, Ed. by Dr. V Kameshwar Rao, Pub. by AY Govt. Archaeology Series

The Hindu Temple- Vol. I by Stella Kramriech

Temples of Tadpatri, by Dr. Ramaswami

Text Book on Geology

Vayupurana Part I, Ed. by Sita Sethstrahidhamy Denbaja

Viśvakṣenasamhita, Ed. by Laxmi Narasiṁha Bhatt, Pub. by Kendriya Sanskrit Vidyapeeth-1972

Viśvakaram Prakāsa, Venkateswara Press, Bombay

Viśvakarama Vāstuśāstram, Ed. by Shri K. Vasudeva Shastri, Pub. by Tanjore Saraswati Mahal Series-1985.

Index